An
AMERICAN SON
Kyler's Journey

C.L. DEVINE
12128 North Division Street, Unit 531
Spokane, WA 99218

Printed in the United States of America

C.L. Devine
An AMERICAN SON: Kyler's Journey
ISBN 978-1-0879-2642-1

First Edition

10 9 8 7 6 5 4 3 2 1

For Apple, Our Journey Continues...

~BASED ON A TRUE STORY~

Kyler Denton has escaped the only world he has ever known. His mother's murderous life has ended. Kyler has nowhere to go and nobody to turn to.

He no longer has to live with the horrendous crimes An American Mom had put him through. Kyler's slate is clean, and he desperately wants to get away from Spokane, Washington.

The memories of Kyler's life haunt him every day. He has no choice but to go searching for answers to his life. Kyler's journey will take him across this great nation.

Come along as Kyler encounters new adventures, more heart-stopping moments and tragedy that will redefine his entire life.

This is Kyler's Journey…

Chapter 1

Leaving Spokane, WA

Sam and I look around at Kenny's empty house. Spokane is a safer place, now that An American Mom, Penny Denton, has passed away. "I'm shocked, it's hard to believe it's over." I said to Sam. "This is it Kyler, let's do this." Sam replied.

I stood there as Sam turned and walked out the front door. I couldn't help but hesitate to leave. It's the end of an era for me. The life, the action, the drama, the murders, it's all over. It's so surreal it makes me light headed.

The fear of the unknown lies ahead. Once I leave this house, there is no turning back. That's a hard pill to swallow, even when I am looking forward to what's ahead of me. "Just take a deep breath, Kyler!" I tell myself.

As I turn towards the front door, I can see my future right in front of me. It's just there, right beyond the threshold of the door. I closed the door and continue walking to freedom.

Sam is right there outside the door, waiting with his usual comical smile. I grabbed his shoulder and said, "Let's go buddy, it's time" "Hi hoe the merry-o!" Sam sang out. We walk to the end of the driveway when Sam asked, "Are we going east or west?

My gut is telling me we should head east. The mountains of Idaho are calling my name. It's been a while since I have been to Idaho, but there is something mysterious about the mountains there.

I turned to Sam, "Let's head east, into Idaho. There is something there calling my name. We should find out what it is." Inspired and motivated, Sam turns to me, "Sounds good, Kyler, let's make way!" We walk down Fourth Ave to Sullivan Road, the last "Main" street we can use to get to Interstate 90.

The traffic isn't very bad this morning. It's a Saturday and still early at six o'clock. Sam and I easily make our way onto Sullivan Road and head south towards the Interstate. We make one last stop at the Chevron gas station to grab two extra bottles of water.

Being outside without a care in the world is the greatest feeling. No direction, no schedule, and nobody to report to. This is my new life and I have to say; I like it. Who knows what adventures we will come across or the people we will meet? As always, we will be very cautious. We are young adults, but we are definitely not stupid. Especially after living with Penny Denton.

You could say I have learned a lesson or two about survival. I can literally sense evil instantly. I will know if a person is on drugs and exactly what their intentions are. Sam is the muscle of the two of us. He will definitely not let anything happen to us.

We make it to Interstate 90, just past the DoubleTree Hotel in Spokane Valley. Sam and I have begun our journey along the interstate. Because we are hitchhiking, this route will increase our chances of getting a ride for various parts of our journey. That and we are not scary looking guys. We are both youthful and clean cut, so we appear safer than your average hitchhiker.

It wasn't too long before we made it to the end of the on-ramp, making our way east towards Idaho. We can safely walk along the interstate using the emergency pull over lane. It was more than wide enough for Sam and I to walk side by side, even with our big hiking packs on.

I look to Sam, "How long do you think it will be before someone picks us up?" Sam turns around to look at the traffic coming from behind us. "Well, the traffic is still light. Our chances may be slim, but as the morning picks up, we might get lucky." Sam was always good with statistics. He could look at a situation and determine the outcome before it happens by using facts and common sense.

The interstate seemed to go on forever. We are covering a respectful distance, but I can tell already we are going to need to take multiple rest stops along the way. My hiking pack is not the lightest thing in the world, but fear not, I can keep up.

I look up and notice a green sign ahead. "Hey look Sam, we have already made it to the Barker exit, that's impressive." I exclaimed. Sam replied, "Hey, before you know it, we will be in Liberty Lake." "There's not much in Liberty Lake, so we should probably not stop there." I suggested.

As we are looking ahead, a red Nissan Sentra pulled off the interstate about thirty feet ahead of us. Sam and I look at each other in shock. "Are they stopping to give us a ride?" I asked Sam. "I don't know Kyler, I'm not the driver, now am I?" He laughed

As we get close to the car, an arm reaches out of the driver's side window, waving us towards them. "They are picking us up, Sam!" I exclaimed. We approach the driver's side door and to our surprise, it is a young lady.

With an enormous smile on her face she asks, "Where are you two headed?" I replied, "We're not sure, kind of just heading out with no direction." "That sounds like fun!" She replied. "I'm headed to the state-line, I can take you that far at least." Sam and I looked at each other and smiled. "We will take it, thank you!"

The young lady opened her trunk for Sam and I to place our hiking packs. We quickly settled in and off we went, driving towards Idaho with a very kind human being.

"My name is Kelly, what are your names?" she asked. I quickly replied, "My name is Kyler, my friend in the back seat is Sam." "It's nice to meet you!" Sam replied. Curious, Kelly asks, "What exactly are you two doing? Do you have a plan?"

I smiled with slight embarrassment, "No, we don't have a plan. We just have our hiking packs and our curiosity to guide our way." She laughed, "You guys are crazy, but that sounds like a ton of fun! I wish I was brave enough to do that."

"Where are you guys going to sleep at night?" She asked. "That's a good question. We'll probably find an out of the way spot to camp for the night. Someplace close to the freeway, but semi-private." I replied. Sam chimed in, "We each have single tents in case the weather is not too great."

As I was about to go into more detail, I see we are turning off the interstate at the state-line of Idaho and Washington. Kelly exclaimed, "Alright boys, I can let you off at the smoke-shop. There are plenty of stores and options to eat breakfast if you guys are hungry." "Sounds great!" I replied.

Kelly drove up to the smoke-shop and popped her trunk. Sam and I got out of the car to retrieve our hiking packs. I grab my pack as Kelly is getting out of her car. "Kelly, thank you again for giving us a wonderful start to our journey." "No problem boys, you take care and stay safe." She replied.

Sam and I put our packs on our back and walked over to the convenience store. This wasn't your regular convenience store to grab a bite to eat. It wasn't a great selection, but at least it was something to put in our bellies. We purchased donuts, bananas, and head outside to sit at one of the tables.

As we are eating our breakfast, we noticed a young couple walking our way. They were as out of place as we are. The young man and woman are also carrying hiking packs on their back. From the looks of things, they appear as if they have been traveling for a while.

The young man has a long, dark beard and ponytail. His skin is tan and weathered. The young woman is also very tan for this time of year. I could tell they may be veteran nomads. They approached and sat at the next table over from us. Sam and I turned and stared, examining their rugged exterior.

We had finished our breakfast and stood up to throw our garbage away. The young man next to us asked, "Hey brother, do you have any leftovers you can spare?" I looked down at the wadded-up napkins, "I'm sorry, we ate it all." I could tell they are starving; you can see it in their faces.

I felt bad for them both, "I am happy to go into the store and get you whatever you would like to eat and something to drink." The young man and woman perked up, "Really, are you serious?" they asked. "Yep, I'm serious, come in the store with me and pick out anything you want." I replied.

The young couple stand up from the table and follow me inside the store. Sam stayed outside to watch everyone's gear. They picked out cold sandwiches, chips,

Gatorade and water. As I stand in line waiting to check out, I can't help but think, "This could happen to us." Sam and I may end up being the ones asking for help throughout our travels.

I always believe in Karma and paying it forward. I'm sure we earned some good points that day. The young man turns around, "Oh yeah, I forgot, my name is Darin and my girlfriend's name is Dena. What's your name?" I replied, "My name is Kyler and my traveling buddy's name is Sam. It's nice to meet you two."

My curiosity has peaked again, "So, which way are you two headed?" I asked Darin and Dena. Darin replied, "We are traveling east towards Montana. We're trying to get to Bozeman, where we grew up. What about you and Sam, where are you going?"

I thought for a second if I should tell them or not. Obviously, we would end up traveling together, since we are headed in the same direction. My gut is telling me they are both safe. "Sam and I are also traveling east. We don't have an official destination yet, just kind of seeing what we see."

Dena asked, "Are you and Sam in a hurry? Would you like to rest for a moment with us since we are going the same way?" I didn't see any harm in that. I know Sam wouldn't care either, "Sure, sounds good!" We got to the checkout counter and paid for their items before we walked back outside.

Once we arrived at the tables, I turned to Sam, "We're going to hang here for a moment while Darin and Dena get situated and eat their breakfast. They are both traveling the same way we are, so I think we may just take off with them when they continue their journey to Bozeman, Montana."

Sam looked over at Darin and Dena, "Sounds great to me, the more the merrier I always say! This is exciting." Sam then asked them, "So tell us why you are trying to get to Bozeman? Do you have family there? Is that where you live?"

Darin and Dena both looked up at us with hesitation. Darin replied, "We have been traveling the United States of America for three years. The roads have taken us thousands of miles across this great nation and we're tired, we are just tired. It's time for us to take a break. We don't have a home in Bozeman, but our childhood friends are still there and they have agreed to let us stay with them until we decided if or when we will do this again."

Dena looked at Darin with a loving smile, "It was all worth it wasn't it though?" Darin replied, "Yes it was babe, yes it was. I am ready for a good night's sleep in an actual bed, though. I have to get off the ground for a while." Darin stated as he laughed.

Sam exclaimed, "Yep, we have a lot to look forward to in the coming days and nights!" "Sam and I are more than happy to tag along with you two all the way to Bozeman." I responded. Darin and Dena looked at each other for a second before Darin responded, "Sure, that sounds great. We can keep each other company."

This is outstanding! We are still in the beginning of our journey and we have found a great couple of people to go along with. I look forward to many more of these encounters throughout our travels. Sam appears to be alright with it. I know when he doesn't like something, he will just come right out and say it.

Darin got up and threw their garbage away, "Dena and I usually find someone at these types of stops that may give us a ride part of the way. So, give us a minute and we will find somebody to get a ride from." I replied, "Awesome! Do your thing, Sam and I will be right here waiting."

Sam and I stayed behind while Darin and Dena wonder off into the parking lot. The store that we are at is also a truck stop and overall last stop before crossing the border east or west. After about ten minutes, Dena comes back, "Hey guys, Darin found somebody that will give us a ride to Superior, Montana. The only thing is, you two will have to ride in the back of his truck, while Darin and I sit up front."

I looked over at Sam, "Sounds good to me, what do you think?" Sam asked, "Isn't that going to be windy? Does he have a canopy or something?" Dena replied, "Oh yeah, sorry, yes, the back of the truck has high wood walls that the owner of the truck built himself. This will block the wind from getting to you both."

The offer was good. Sam replied, "Ok, let's do it!" I couldn't believe it; Sam is taking a leap into the unknown. For a typically well researched individual, he doesn't seem to mind the spontaneity of the situation.

We then see Darin come around the corner in the passenger seat of an old Ford pickup truck. Dena wasn't kidding when she said he had wood walls on the side. They are six feet by five-feet pieces of plywood that have are attached to the guard rails on the bed of the truck. I could tell the wind would not affect us too much. I could tell Sam is ok with it as well because he is still smiling.

The driver is an older gentleman who appears to be a farmer his entire life. He is just as leathery looking as Darin and Dena. The sun can really do a number on you. Sam and I place our hiking packs in the back of the truck and climb in. We sit near the front of the truck with our backs to the rear window. The high wood walls provided great protection from the wind.

Suddenly, I hear an old man's voice, "Alright, hold on!" We drive towards the interstate where we will continue our journey across this nation. I could tell when we got on the freeway because the truck instantly picked up speed. Sam and I could hear the roar of the wind going over the truck, but we didn't feel it too much.

I grabbed my hiking pack and leaned it up against the side of the truck. I then leaned over on it to use it as a giant pillow of some sorts. Sam watched what I was doing. He grabbed his hiking pack and did the same thing. "Great idea!" Sam stated. We might as well get comfortable, it's going to be a couple hours' drive to Superior, Montana.

Overall, the ride wasn't horrible. Yes, it was bumpy, but the nice man who is driving us is attempting to avoid any bumps or potholes. Sam and I are safe from the elements and hidden from view of any passing motorists. Mostly, it was a great deal.

I looked over at Sam and asked, "Did you think it was going to start out this way? I'm not sure how we have done it, but we seem to meet the right people at the right time." Sam stared towards the rear of the truck bed for a moment, "You know, you are right, Kyler! How did all of this happen?"

When you look at it from our perspective, it is better to have some luck than no luck at all. Our gut instincts are leading us in the right direction so far. "Sam, thank you for coming along with me. This wouldn't have been as fun if I was by myself."

Sam smiled and replied, "I wouldn't miss it for the world. How could I not go along on this once in a lifetime experience?" I'm relieved Sam feels this way. When I make life choices, I try not to be an inconvenience to anybody around me.

Chapter 2

Unlucky Lil's

We continued east on Interstate 90, heading towards Superior, Montana. It wouldn't be long before we will pull off the freeway. Sam and I got our hiking packs together and sat up, preparing ourselves to offload from the truck. Then I hear a knocking sound. I turned around towards the truck's rear window. Dena is signaling to us we are pulling off.

I'm partly relieved to get out of the truck. Although grateful for the ride, being skinny and laying on bare metal is not always the most comfortable things to do. It's bones on metal, but no bother, it's about to be over.

The last stage of the ride gets bumpier as we pull off the interstate. Suddenly, the squeaking of the breaks becomes louder as we come to a stop.

Sam and I jump up, grab our hiking packs and head to the rear of the truck bed. The nice old man came around and let the tailgate down. We hop off the back and inspect around. "Not bad!" I tell Sam. "Hey, we are at Lucky Lil's Casino!" Sam replies. "It looks small", I responded.

Sam is happy to advise me on his knowledge of Lucky Lil's Casino, "It's a chain of small casinos that attached to gas stations and trucks stops along highways and interstates. No one really wins a lot of money here. But it's a fun way to pass the time."

Darin and Dena make their way to the back of the truck, to Sam and I. The nice old man who drove us here has already gone inside the casino. Darin asked, "Before we go inside to get something to drink, would you both like to step around back for a small joint?"

Sam's eyes opened wide as his smile grew, "Yeah, you bet, let's go! Kyler, are you coming?" I was hesitant at first, "I'll go with you guys, sure, why not?" We all walked around behind the casino near the back dumpster. There was no one around as Darin pulled the joint out of this backpack.

"Fire it up!" Darin exclaimed as he handed the joint to Dena. "Ladies first as always", she replied. Sam waited anxiously for his turn; he really loves weed.

13

Anytime he has time to smoke, he takes it. I am a lightweight, some would say.

Dena took a nice long hit to get the joint started. The weed smells fantastic. I can tell it's not the cheap brown bud with seeds and stems. Dena coughed hard as she passed the joint to Sam. Darin blurted out, "That's the hydroponic right there, boys!"

Sam took a nice long hit of the joint. The more he dragged on the joint, the wider his eyes got. Suddenly a plume of smoke ejected from Sam's mouth. He is ravishingly coughing all over the place. I quickly grab the joint out of his unsteady hands as he attempts to pass it to me under convulsions.

I laughed out loud asking Sam, "Are you ok buddy? Did you take a little too much of the wacky weed?" Darin and Dena laughed so hard as Sam attempted to catch his breath. "Oh my god! What is that?" Sam squelched.

Darin proudly replied, "This is the sticky of the icky, icky! It's the one-hitter-quitter, and I got you!" My hit of the joint is slow to make sure I don't throw up my lungs like Sam did. I can feel the power of this weed immediately. I quickly pass the joint to Darin as I cough.

I look over at Sam and laugh. His eyes are already squinty and red. He has officially transformed into slow motion. I didn't take as big of a hit as Sam, so I am still functioning well, even though I feel relaxed. What I would like to do is get a bottle of water and sit down somewhere. "Should we go inside?" I asked.

Dena perked up, "That sounds like a great idea. We could all probably use some water right about now." Trying to maintain our balance, we all slowly stood up to gain our bearings. Everything around us looked and sounded different. The surrounding colors are more vibrant and the sounds are enhanced as if we could hear everything. This is definitely the work of the weed.

We walk inside the store and we were hit with a blast of air conditioning that woke us right up. Dena walks over to the cooler to grab four bottles of water. "Water is on me, I will take care of this one since you guys smoked with us", I said as we approached the check-out counter. "Thanks, man! We appreciate that!" Darin replied.

I handed the bottles of water to everyone and we walked back outside. I kind of wanted to try my hand at the slots inside Lucky Lil's Casino, so I asked, "Hey, do you all want to go inside the casino and see what happens with five dollars each? I'll pay for it." Sam immediately replied, "Heck yeah! Let's do it!" Darin and Dena looked at each other than replied, "You bet, why not? It couldn't hurt to try!"

We all walked around to the other side of the building to the casino. It is small inside, but packed with slot machines. I'm wonder how a chain of casino's like this could stay in business. Could they really afford to pay out big money in such a small place? Who knows? Let's have some fun.

I handed everyone five dollars each, and we dispersed to find our lucky slot machines. It's not like we could go very far. The casino is about as big as a convenience store. I used my gut instinct to find the right slot machine. Not saying that would work, but it is worth a try.

While walking down the aisle, I come to a machine called Four Alarm Fire. It had a picture of a building on fire with firefighters scrambling to put out the flames. I thought, "Well, this one looks as good as any!" I sat down and put my five-dollar bill into the machine. I'm stoned and excited with anticipation that I might win a couple dollars, but probably not. I'm sure I am just donating five dollars to the casino.

Out of nowhere, someone sat down at the machine just to the right of me. I look over to see a smiling older woman staring at my machine's screen. She is beautiful. You could tell she just had her hair done and her makeup was flawless. I said, "Hi there! How are you?" The lady replied, "I'm good! Are you winning any big money?"

I responded, "Not yet, I just started playing. I'm sure I will lose my entire five-dollars." She reached over and placed her hand over mine on the buttons of the machine. "Here, I will help you!" she exclaimed with a flirtatious smile on her face. So, not only do I immediately freeze up because someone is touching me without my permission, but she is staring deep into my eyes as if she can read my soul. I am shocked that an African American woman in her thirties, who probably weighs over two hundred fifty pounds with short blond hair, would even be remotely interested in my scrawny Caucasian ass. Can you see how this appears to be an awkward situation?

I quickly look around for Sam, Darin or Dena, but they are nowhere in view. I can hear them, but I cannot see them. The woman grabs my face and turns my head in her direction. "Are you going to buy me a drink?" she asked. Feeling somewhat frightened, I replied, "Sure, what would you like?" "I'll take a whiskey with Coke", she responded.

This is my opportunity to break hold of her grip on my hand. I jumped up and said, "Great, I will be right back!" I quickly waked away in search of Sam. There is no way I want to be left alone with that woman. She appears as if she could eat me alive, and I'm not down with that. I turn the corner to see Sam at a nickel machine. He has a big smile on his face, so he must do well.

I ran as fast as I could over to Sam as he looked over to see me coming towards him. I grabbed him by the shoulder and said, "Dude, you will not believe what just happened to me!" Sam replied, "What? Did you win big money?" I replied, "No Sam, this lady just came up to me and started touching me and flirting with me. Now she wants me to buy her a drink! Come over there with me!"

Sam got up out of his seat and walked to the end of the aisle. He slowly crept around the corner until he could see down the other aisle. Sam quickly jerked back and stared at me with his eyes almost bulging out of his head. "Dude! Are you kidding me?" he laughed. Sam ran back to me in hysterics. "How on earth could that lady possibly think you are attractive? Look at you! You are a white, skinny bean pole!"

On that note, I agreed with Sam. How in this universe could this be happening? "I have to get her drink fast before she comes looking for me." I run over to the bar and order her drink. Ice, whiskey, Coke and done. The bartender hands me the drink and I pass him a five-dollar bill. I grab the drink and walk fast back to the woman without spilling a drop.

I get back to the slot machine and hand her the drink. She is still playing on my original five-dollar investment. I look at the screen. To my amazement, she is up to twenty-seven dollars. "That's great!" I exclaimed. "You bet, honey! I know my machines!" she replied. "What is your name?" I asked. "My name is Kim, nice to meet you honey!" "I'm Kyler, it's nice to me you."

Just then, Sam comes around the corner and sits to the left of me. "Hey guys, what's happening?" he asked. I replied, "Sam this Kim, Kim this is Sam!" "It's great to me you!" Sam responded. "Likewise," Kim replied. She stared into Sam's eyes in the same flirtatious way that she did to me. Sam's eyes widened as he smiled back at Kim.

Out of nowhere, I hear Dena yell out, "Woo Hoo! Oh my god!" Daren came racing around the corner to us. "You guys, Dena won one hundred and forty dollars! I can't believe it!" he screamed out as he ran back to Dena. Sam and I smiled and yelled out, "Great job, you guys! That's awesome!" Then the unbelievable happened.

As I am sitting there celebrating Darin and Dena's new found fortune, Kim grabbed my right hand. Without hesitation, she places my hand down her shirt and inside her bra. I quickly jerked my hand back and exclaimed,

"Oh, no thank you! I'm good." Kim replied, "Are you sure, baby? I'll charge you twenty dollars." Right then, I knew what Kim was.

I turn to Sam and tap him on the shoulder. "It's time to go, Sam. We need to get on the road." I motioned to Sam in a discrete manner that we need to leave now. He picked up on what I am trying to say and replied, "Oh yeah, you are right, we should go." We both got up, turned to Kim and said, "Well, it was great to meet you. We have to go now."

Kim responded, "Ok boys, you have a safe trip. If you come back this way, be sure to look me up. I am always her looking for a good time." Sam and I turned and walked back to Darin and Dena. As soon as we got to them, I motioned for them to huddle together. I whispered, "You guys won't believe it! That lady on the other side is a prostitute. I could see the signs from a mile away. She propositioned me, but I turned her down."

Darin, Dena, and Sam all laughed hysterically. "Let's get out of here!" I advised. Darin and Dena went to the bartender to cash out their winnings. Sam and I walked outside while we waited. I turned to Sam, "I will never forget Kim! I cannot believe that happened to me!" I am still dumbfounded, as you can tell. Sam replied, "Dude, she would have taken you for everything you have! You are lucky we got out of there when we did!"

It wasn't long before Darin and Dena came out of the casino with their winnings. Darin exclaimed, "Here you guys, here is twenty-dollars for each of you. You guys fed us, gave us something to drink, and provided the five-dollars that allowed us to win this money. We can't thank you enough!" Dena smiled and said, "Yes, thank you both! You are our life-savers today!"

Sam and I are happy to help. I replied, "How fitting is this? Sam and I are just starting our journey as you two are ending yours. This couldn't have been any better. What are you going to do now?" Darin replied, "Well, we now have enough money to take the Greyhound bus the rest of the way home. Would you and Sam like to join us? They sell the bus tickets inside the convenience store and the bus will pick us up right here at this truck stop."

Wanting to stay in budget I asked, "How much are the tickets to get us from here to Bozeman, Montana?" Dena replied, "They are super cheap, only twenty-dollars! You can use the twenty dollars that we just gave you."

She is right. The next leg of our trip wouldn't cost us any money since we would use the cash, they just gave us. "Sound like a deal!" I responded. Sam and I walked inside and purchased our tickets. The next bus would come in about thirty minutes, so that's isn't too bad. Darin chimed in, "Hey guys, let's go for a quick walk around back to the trees and finish that joint.

Sam replied, "I'm down! We will be on a bus so that would be perfect!" I responded, "Sure, let's go!" All four of us walked around back and disappeared into the woods. It really is a peaceful experience smoking weed in the woods. The sights and sounds of the forest become extra vibrant.

Chapter 3

Roadkill Highway

After emerging from the woods, we only had to wait another ten minutes before the bus would arrive. I thought to myself, "I have plenty of time to go back inside the convenience store, use the restroom and get something to drink." We all walked back inside to sit at a booth in the air conditioning while we waited.

I sat my hiking pack down to use the restroom and grab another drink before boarding the bus. Darin, Dena and Sam all gathered what they needed and sat back in the booth to wait for the bus. It appears as if we got a little too caught up in our conversation. It felt as if only a couple minutes had gone by before they announced that the bus was about to leave.

We all four looked at each other in shock. "How can that be? We didn't even hear them announce the bus was here!" I exclaimed as we got up in a rush. "Let's go Kyler!" Sam yelled as I was placing my hiking pack on my back.

Darin bolted through the front door, holding it open for the rest of us as we ran outside. Thank goodness the bus is still there. I was the first to make it to the bus's door. I stared up at the driver as he gave me the look of death. He reminded me of a drill instructor for the military, right down to the high and tight haircut and the Smokey the Bear hat. I could see him saying something to the rest of the passengers. I could only imagine he is making a comment about us being late for the bus.

The driver finally opened the bus door and immediately exclaimed, "You're all late!" I quickly replied, "We are so sorry, we didn't hear the announcement that the bus was here!" We all quickly boarded the bus and handed the driver out tickets. I turn around to see a half full bus of people staring at us in shame. All I could do is awkwardly smile as we made our way to the back of the bus.

As soon as we made it to our seats, we were hit with the smells of the bus. You never realize how many humans use the bathroom until you have to take the Greyhound. It's basically one giant porta-potty on wheels. We didn't have a lot of room to store our things so we packed them in as much as possible in the overhead compartments.

I asked Sam, "Can I sit by the window?" Sam replied, "Go for it buddy, I will probably have to use the bathroom more than you, anyway. I'll take the aisle seat." I enjoy staring out the window at the passing landscape. It also helps keep my ADHD occupied. I can't just sit here staring at the back of the seat in front of me. That's enough to drive a person crazy.

The driver pulls away on to Interstate 90 and drives east to our next destination, Bozeman, Montana. I look over to see Darin and Dena going through their belongings getting ready for their final destination. My eyes scan the rest of the bus. I am a people watcher. I am always curious to see what people look like in different settings. The Greyhound bus is a perfect people watching experience if you can handle the smells.

Sam grabs his headphones and compact disc player. Before we left, he burned a mixed music cd for the road. In our day, music is an important part of our life. Everything we do had something to do with music. I stared out the window at the scenery.

We are at the part of Montana where the trees disappear and you begin to see hillsides and fields of grass for miles to come. The other interesting part was the blood-stained highway. I couldn't help but notice the amount of roadkill strewn about the highway.

I had never seen so many bloody dead animal carcasses in my life. I couldn't help but think, "Isn't there a roadkill cleanup division of the Department of

Transportation?" You would think there should be with the large number of dead animals on the highway. The driver maneuvered around them. I can only assume that he is used to it.

A lot of this is new to me. I am so excited to see new towns and meet new people. I can't tell you how much I am looking forward to so many new experiences. I have to find out what the rest of the country has to offer. Is it possible that I may make my home somewhere else besides Spokane, Washington? If so, where will it be?

I keep looking up at the green highway signs to always know where we are at all times. I can't help but wonder how these towns got their names. For instance, we just passed Alberton, Montana. If you blinked, you sure as hell missed it. Who named that town? Was it a guy name Albert? Well, come to find out, it was named after a guy named Albert Earling. He was the president of the Chicago, Milwaukee, St. Paul and Pacific Railroad.

Next, we have Frenchtown, Montana. This town is interesting. It's about 20 times bigger than Alberton, but still a small town. The settlement was founded around 1858 by two French Canadians moving inland with their Metis families, to escape turmoil further west, that followed the arrival of the American federal authorities. Very interesting. It's crazy to think of what people had to go through during that time.

The city name that we just passed made me laugh. The sign said, "Wye, Montana!" That had me busting up. Why are we asking Wye, Montana? I laughed so hard.

There's only around three hundred people who live here and I wonder if they are asking themselves, "Wye?"

Our first pickup and rest stop are coming up. We are about to enter Missoula, Montana. The second largest city in Montana after Billings. I had been to Missoula once when I was a child. I traveled here with my mom's friend Candy and some guy that had a crush on her. He didn't realize he was helping her transport drugs, but I'm pretty sure we covered that already.

The driver pulls off the interstate and into Missoula, Montana. You can see the history in this town, it's everywhere. This is like your typical storybook town, a place you could safely raise your family. The Greyhound station isn't very close to the interstate, so we have to drive through town for a moment.

I could see we are coming upon the Clark Fork River as the bus slows down. The bus station in Missoula is more of a bus stop instead of a bus station. It's a tiny brick building with a parking lot. To the untrained eye, it would appear to be a rest stop of some sort.

We came to a stop in the parking lot. The driver announced, "You have twenty minutes to use the restroom and stretch your legs. Do not wander off. We will leave on time, with or without you." I was like, "Wow, that's kind of harsh! I bet it gets the point across though.

We all step off the bus and take a deep breath of fresh Montana air. It's so beautiful! Missoula is surrounded by amazing mountains. I am so jealous at this moment. The people of this city get to see this every day. Spokane has hills, but we don't have these types of large mountains this close in view. I really am a nature person deep down inside.

It would be great to walk down to the river, but we wouldn't be able to make it back in time. Darin asked, "What do you guys want to do?" Sam looked around and replied, "I don't know. Where kind of trapped here on this side by a busy street. There's no way we can make it to the river and back in time."

I look down the street, "Well, I don't see much either. It may be a good idea to hang out here, just in case. I don't want to miss the bus like we did in at the casino." Everybody agreed with me. Darin and Dena are so close to finally making it home, they do not want to risk messing that up.

So, we did what any other young adult would do while traveling across the country. We watched as the bus driver went inside his private break room and we walked across the parking lot behind the empty building next door to smoke a joint. Of course, this was Darin's idea. I'm a lightweight, so I was still fine from the casino, but I guess I could try one more.

There was a nice summer breeze going as we huddled together behind the small building. Darin lit the joint to get it started. It wasn't long before we had all had our turn. One round is enough for me. I am probably one hundred thirty-five pounds so it doesn't take much to make me relaxed.

We hung out there in the shade until it was time to go back. We could hear the scrambling of people walking towards the bus a few minutes before departure. It is time to head out. The bus driver started the bus as we made our way back. Dena had sprayed us all with her body spray to mask the smell of the marijuana. We didn't want any trouble during our travels.

The bus was still not packed. I would say maybe only three quarters full as we left Missoula, Montana. It was great because there weren't so many people it made the trip uncomfortable. As we got back in our seats, I asked Darin and Dena, "Are you two excited to get home?" Darin replied, "You bet, we will be there soon. I can't wait to walk through that front door and head straight to the restroom to take a shower!"

Dena responded, "It will be nice to have a stable place while we get things sorted out. I can't wait to sleep in my own bed again!" I could tell they had been on the road for a long time. I wonder when I will get to that point of return. When will my body say, "Hey, it's time to go home and rest!" We will see, I guess.

As we were talking about their new life, a passenger came running down the aisle to the bathroom. You could tell they must have had to go really bad. After a couple seconds, we could all hear exactly how bad it really was. That poor person must have eaten something bad at the last stop. I could tell, it was not a good scene in there.

After fifteen minutes the exhausted lady emerged from the restroom. It only took a half second for the entire bus to be attacked by the smell of her aftermath. We all covered our noses and mouths quickly as Dena grabbed for her purse. She reached in and pulled out her bod spray

27

and began spraying all over the place. Everybody opened their windows to not throw up on the bus.

The lady knew she did wrong, but there was no stopping her emergency. We all had to sit and suffer until the airflow from the open windows could clear out the bus. We definitely made sure the restroom door was closed tight. I kept my shirt over my nose and mouth for a good thirty minutes before I could trust that the smell had dissipated.

Sam could not stop laughing as he took his hand away from his face. "Oh my god!" he exclaimed. Darin and Dena looked over at us. Dena asked, "Are you guys ok?" This is so funny. We are acting as if we got attacked or something. Oh, how funny? I replied, "Yes, we are ok. I think we are going to make it!"

With only an hour to go until we are in Bozeman, Darin and Dena are getting their gear together. They have all of their bags in order. Darin called his brother and let him know to head over to the bus station to pick them up. You could tell they are both relieved.

Bozeman is also a change-over city. This means that some travelers will get off the bus and new ones will board. I notice that I get anxiety wondering who the new people will be. As they board the bus, all I can think is, "Please don't stink! I know that sounds odd, but I really don't like it when people forget how to use deodorant.

We kicked back and relaxed the rest of the way to Bozeman, Montana. Sam had his cd player going with his headphones on. Darin and Dena are cuddled up with each other across the aisle. That leaves me, I am just staring out the window watching the world go by. At least for this moment, the world consists of grain silos and small trailers from the 1970s.

I noticed a trend as we made our way into Bozeman. I had never seen so many abandoned cars parked around one person's trailer before. Every few miles there would be someone's trailer home with a dozen or more abandoned cars parked outside. It's almost as if they are a collection or being sold for parts. Who knows? It is fascinating to see though.

It wasn't long before the driver announced that we are pulling into Bozeman, Montana. This is a different feeling for two reasons. The first, we are saying goodbye to Darin and Dena, but the second is that we are entering the birthplace of An American Mom, Penny Denton. Yes, that's right, my mom was born right here in Bozeman, Montana and decades later, here I am. What a strange world.

Darin and Dena get up out of their seats to grab their gear from the overhead compartments. I told Sam, "Hey, let's grab our stuff, this is our stop!" Sam and I have to decide what to do. It's still early in the day that we could still get some traveling done. We might catch a ride with someone as we head east on foot. I guess we will have to see how good our luck is going to be.

Sam got up and grabbed our hiking packs. He handed mine to me as he placed swung his around to his back. It feels great to stand up after having to sit in a cramped bus seat for hours at a time. You can only take so much of this before you have to get off the bus and stretch your legs.

The driver pulls into the bus station and we are all ready to get off the bus. Mostly it wasn't too bad, just a little claustrophobic. It felt great to stretch my legs and take a deep breath of that fresh northwest air. Darin and Dena noticed their brother waiting by his car so it is time to say goodbye.

Darin stated, "Hey, it was great to meet you guys. Thank you for helping us in our time of need! If it wasn't for you two, we would still be hiking our way home! Dena and I are forever grateful." I replied, "No problem my friend. It was great to meet you guys too!" "Take care!" Sam replied.

They both ran to their brother's car as Sam and I took a good look around. It just after two in the afternoon so we have plenty of daylight to make it a good distance to our next destination. I turned to Sam, "Let's take a break over here on this bench while we think of our next move."

As we sat on the bench eating some snacks, I asked Sam, "Where should we go next?" Sam replied, "Well, we could keep going along the interstate to Billings, Montana. Is there anything on your bucket list that you want to see while we are headed that way?

I thought for a moment before replying, "I would really like to see Mount Rushmore! I have never been to a national monument before and I would be honored for that one to be my first!" Sam replied, "Let's do it! Why not? I would like to see Mount Rushmore. What do you say we finish our snacks and head on out? There are plenty of fields to camp in if we are still on the road overnight."

I took one more drink of water before grabbing my hiking pack. "Well, there's no better time than now! Let's go!" Sam and I walked our trek back to the interstate. It took a good half hour to get back on I-90 from the bus station. I am glad to be back in nature, breathing the fresh air of freedom. Anything is better than having to breathe whatever is on the bus, that is for sure.

Sam and I headed east down the interstate. We didn't have our thumbs out yet. We really wanted to take in the country side and enjoy walking the trails of another state. As much as we were enjoying it, our vehicle bound travelers seemed to have a different idea.

Chapter 4

Old Montana

I was just looking over at the mountainside when a truck half full of hay, pulled off the road just ahead of us. The driver poked his head out the window and yelled, "Hey, you guys need a lift?" Sam and I looked at each other and shrugged our shoulders. "Why not?" Sam said. I replied, "Sure, let's do it." We both ran to the driver's side of the man's truck.

The old man in the driver's seat yelled out, "Jump in back! I'm going as far as Billings and that's it!" "That's perfect!" I replied. I turned to Sam, "Hop in back, let's go!" We both jumped into the back of the truck with our hiking packs. This is great! I have always wanted to go on a hay ride and I guess this is the same thing, right?

We placed our packs down and rested against the hay. "It doesn't get any better than this does it, Sam?" Sam laughed, "You bet buddy, you bet!" You could tell we are both having the time of our lives. We are hundreds of miles away from home and already having a blast. Who knows what will happen next?

Billings, Montana is about an hour and a half away so Sam and I got comfortable. We are learning early to get as much sleep as possible. We both lied down to take a quick nap. This was also to hide amongst the hay from passing motorists. The wind was howling while we were in the back, but we had no problem falling asleep for an hour.

We woke to find ourselves near our destination. Sam and I grabbed our drinks to fully wake up out of our slumber. I looked around. Yep, same thing. Trailers with dozens of cars and plenty of roadkill to go around. I am so fascinated with this concept. That's ok, this is what we signed up for.

The old man pulled off the interstate and drove for a short distance before pulling into the parking lot of the Cracker Barrel Old Country Store. I couldn't believe it. I had only heard others talk of the Cracker Barrel but I had never seen it in person. All these years of seeing their cheese and food products in the grocery stores and now I am at their actual location. This has to be a bucket list check off for me.

Sam has a one-track mind, "Do you think they have food in there?" I replied, "Yes Sam, it's a restaurant as well as a store. If you are hungry, let's go inside and look around." We both hopped out of the back of the truck to the waiting driver. "Thank you, sir! Is there any way we can repay you?" I asked. The old man replied, "No, thank you! I traveled around when I was your age, so it's nice to see you kids keeping the dream alive! Take care and watch each other's back!" That was a cryptic thing to say, but alright.

We both walk inside Cracker Barrel for the first time. This is history in the making for me. Sam and I walked through the front doors to see exactly what is on the sign outside. It is literally an old country store. This is amazing. I feel like I just walked back in time. Apart from the modern-day salt and pepper shakers, this place is pretty authentic.

Alright, so the Cracker Barrel has lived up to its hype so far, but we need to try the food. They young female host found us a corner table to sit our hiking packs down and out of the way. I couldn't take my eyes off the ceiling and walls. I literally felt like I was having flashbacks to the mid-1800s even though I wasn't alive during that time.

Sam and I ordered the best southern fried chicken and the pot pie. We will share this as it appears to be more than enough for two people. I can tell you this, they did not disappoint on the food or the overall experience. I recommend the Cracker Barrel to anyone passing through Billings, Montana.

After eating our meal, Sam asked, "So what should we do now?" I thought for a second, "Well, I guess we could stroll on down the road until it gets dark. We can pull off into a field or trees to set up our tents right before it gets dark."

Sam agreed as we paid our bill and made our way outside with our hiking packs. The sun was extra bright after leaving the lightly lit inside of the Cracker Barrel. Sam and I head towards the interstate. Our next destination will be Mount Rushmore.

To get to Mount Rushmore, we have to travel over three hundred miles east of where we currently are. It could take us a week or it could take us less than a day, it depends on how we get there. For now, we are getting there on foot.

Sam and I make it to the interstate and begin our trek. "This is pretty awesome Kyler!" Sam exclaimed. "I know Sam, I wouldn't have it any other way! The freedom to go wherever you want whenever you want is something, I never want to give back." Sam replied, "We have no clue where this is going to take us. I hope we find what we are both looking for." "I hope so!" I responded.

The view of mountains ahead is intimidating and beautiful at the same time. We are definitely grateful for those that came before us for carving this path ahead. "Hey, look what I found!" Sam shouted out. I turned around to see him holding four joints in his hand. "Where did you get those?" I asked. Sam replied, "I forgot, Darin gave them to me before we left Bozeman, Montana."

After looking around, I said, "Well, light one up! What are you waiting for?" Sam reached into his pocket and grabbed his lighter. With the flick of his thumb, he lit up a joint. I am surprised we could smoke a joint and dodge the roadkill at the same time. It was quite impressive.

As we were walking along the interstate, I could see something moving in the distance. I squinted my eyes to get a better look. "Sam!" I blurted out. "Look, are hose horses up ahead?" Sam looked up in surprise, "I think so! Yes, those are horses. Oh my gosh, we get to see some horses!" You can tell we are both quite stoned, but we love horses.

We both pick up our pace, but not too fast since we don't want to scare the horses away. It wasn't too long before we were right at their fence. The only thing that separated us was a barbwire fence and tall grass. The horses didn't seem to be bothered by use. I walked up to the fence to pet the horse, but it backed away a few inches out of reach. I was ok with that, look but don't touch.

I asked Sam, "Hey, take a picture of me and the horse." Sam reached into his pack and pulled out his disposable Kodak camera. "Hold on, I need to wind the film first!" he yelled. After winding the disposable camera Sam replied, "Ok, stand in front of the horse. I stood in front of the horse while Sam took the picture. Luckily, the horses were not bothered by the flash on the camera.

Sam walked down to the fence, walked right up to the horse and started petting him. "What! That's not fair! How come the horse is letting you pet him and not me?" Sam replied, "You just have to tell them who is boss Kyler!" I walked over to the horse to pet him and the horse pulled away. "Forget it!" I said, "Let's just go!"

Sam laughed as he pets the horse one more time before we left. I wanted to keep moving to find a good spot to camp before dark. Sam caught up to me as we continued down the interstate. "I want a copy of those pictures. We will have to find a one-hour photo somewhere to get them developed." Sam replied, "No problem, we can find a drug store with one of those in any bigger town.

After walking for five hours, we are just passing Toluca, Montana. Toluca is one of those towns that you can miss if you blink, even if you are walking. The next city ahead is Hardin, Montana. I think we should stop somewhere for the night. The sun is about to go down and we still need to set up our tents.

We walk off the interstate into a field of grass. "I think it would be best to camp by a couple trees, just in case we need the extra shelter above us." Sam replied, "I agree and I see some right over there!" Sam spotted a bundle of trees next to a small hill in out in a field. It appeared to be easy to get to as it is just off of a side gravel road.

This is perfect! We made it to the camp spot. It is like an oasis on the farm. Such a perfect set up for an overnight stay. Sam and I quickly put up our single-man tents. Next, we set up a fire pit with our cooking utensils. It is time to make some dinner.

Tonight, we are having a traditional cook out meal. Hot dogs, with pork and beans that I bought from the convenience store at the casino. This is a perfect time to eat them. I asked Sam, "Hey, can you grab the two tin cups off of my backpack? I made us some tea." Sam grabbed the tin cups, "Here you go, sir!"

We sat and ate our dinner next to the campfire under the twilight sky. This is such an amazing memory in history. How often can you say that you ate a campfire dinner in the middle of a field in Montana? Not very many can.

As we sat there talking about our plans for the morning, I suddenly saw a pair of headlights coming down the interstate. It had been a while since we had seen anyone. Strange thing is, this truck looks like it is slowing down towards the road we walked down to get to our camp site.

I watched as the trucked slowed down and turned onto our road. Whoever was driving is coming towards us with a purpose. "Sam, check it out!" I said as I pointed towards the truck. "Uh oh!" Sam replied, "Are we in trouble?" he asked. "I don't think so. There shouldn't be any harm in what we are doing unless we are on private land."

The truck came to a stop just across from us at the road. We watched as a young lady got out of the truck and walked towards our camp. "Hello boys! Do you know where you are at?" she asked. As she comes closer, I get a better look. She appears to be a young Native American woman in her mid-twenties.

I replied, "I think so. Are we on private property?" She replied, "No and yes! It is not safe you two here! You boys are on the Crow Reservation. Do you have any idea what can happen to a couple of white guys like you if you are caught out here camping?"

I looked at Sam with a bit of fear, "Um, well... I guess we should go then, right Sam?" Sam looked at the young lady, "Yes, you bet, we are going to pack up right now and get the hell out of here!" The young lady looked at us and laughed as we scurried around to breakdown our camp site.

I put the fire out as Sam packed up our tents and sleeping bags. The young lady instructed, "Put your stuff in the back of my truck, I will take you out of here to a safe place." I looked over at Sam for his approval. He seemed to be okay with it as he walked towards her truck with the gear. After placing everything in the truck's bed, the young woman stated, "Hop in the back, let's go!"

Sam and I hoped in the back of the truck, thankful to be alive. I turned to Sam, "I am not sure what she meant by our safety, but I am convinced she is looking out for our best interests." Sam nodded his head, "I agree my friend, I agree. I think we were just saved by an angel."

We can't really see where we are going since it is pitch black outside. In this area of Montana, there aren't exactly any street lights around. Suddenly, Sam and I could see the lights of what looks to be a motel. I'm not sure what road we are on, but it's the only structure in sight. Wouldn't you know it! She took us to a Best Western.

The young lady pulls into the parking lot and comes to a stop. Sam and I jump out of the back of the truck as she exits the driver side. "Ok boys, here we are! Grab your stuff, let's go inside!" she instructed. I quickly replied, "Wait a second, we weren't planning on paying for a hotel, that is why we're camping."

She turned around and said, "Look boys, I have saved you from what could have been your certain death. It's on me, I own this damn hotel! Now grab your shit and get inside!" Sam and I looked at each other in shock. We didn't waste time as we grabbed our gear and followed her inside.

I am curious how a person so young could own a hotel. We went inside and up to the front desk. "My name is Mountain Flower." She stated. I replied, "My name is Kyler, and this is Sam. We are traveling across country." "It's nice to meet you Mountain Flower,", Sam replied. "How do you own this hotel?" I asked.

Mountain Flower replied, "First, I live on a reservation. Second, I wanted to start a business, so the government gave me a grant to get me started. If you are a female minority, the government will throw money at you to start a business. So, there you go boys! Here is your room key. You sharing a room with two full size beds."

I am super impressed, "Thank you so much Mountain Flower! Thank you for potentially saving our lives and giving us shelter." Sam added, "Yes, thank you for taking care of us." As we walked away, Mountain Flower replied, "Hey, be down here by seven in the morning for a continental breakfast!" I replied, "Oh, we will, I promise!"

Sam and I walked to our room on the first floor. This was great, no elevator to take. I can't believe we get went from camping in a field to staying in a hotel room in less than an hour. We are definitely super lucky. Sometimes I think someone is watching over us.

After taking showers, Sam and I settled in with a couple snacks and some television. You never know when the next time we will watch TV. "Are you having fun so far Sam?" I asked. "You bet my friend!" Sam replied. I added, "This is a once in a lifetime thing and we are doing it. I can't believe it!" Sam replied, "I can't believe it either. I am happy to be along for the ride!"

Chapter 5

The Great Monument

The hotel was silent that night. Sam and I could get just the right amount of sleep to recharge our internal batteries. We both woke up at 6:30 am the next morning. Just enough time for us to each take a shower and get downstairs in time to enjoy the continental breakfast.

After stuffing our faces and filling our bellies, we were greeted with a familiar face. Mountain Flower came by our table to check on us. "How were your overnight stays boys?" Mountain Flower asked. I replied with a big smile, "You have an amazing hotel here. We both enjoyed our stay." Sam chimed in, "Thank you for the breakfast, this was exactly what we needed before we hit the road."

"Where are you headed today?" Mountain Flower asked. "We would like to see Mount Rushmore since we are within hitch hiking distance," I replied. "Both of us have never been there," Sam added. "That's quite the distance. You're looking at five to six hours of driving time. Who knows how long it will take you to get there in between rides, if you can find one?" Mountain Flower stated.

Our curiosity perked up. We both looked up at Mountain Flower as she continued, "Listen boys, even though it is daylight there is still a chance you may get in to the wrong vehicle around here," I asked, "How do we get out of here safely then?" "You two wait right here. I'll check around and find someone who is driving in direction of Mount Rushmore." She replied.

Sam and I waited patiently while Mountain Flower searched the hotel for anyone heading east. We truly never expected a person to be so nice and accommodating. After coming from Spokane, it sure is a nice to meet good people out here on the road. So far, Sam and I have been very lucky.

Within a half hour, Mountain Flower returned with somebody by her side. "Boys, I would like you to meet Kelly." "Hi Kelly, my name is Kyler, and this is Sam" I advised. "Kelly is heading east and would be happy to have you along for the ride" Mountain Flower exclaimed. "That's amazing!" I happily replied.

Kelly stated, "Let's grab your things and hit the road. It's going to be a long drive, but we should be there within 6 hours at the most." Sam and I hopped out of our seats to grab our things. "I call shotgun" Sam replied. That is perfectly fine with me. If Kelly has a car with a nice backseat, I could catch some sleep during the drive. I didn't tell Sam that just in case he had the same idea. Even though we had a good night sleep, I was still tired, especially after eating such a big breakfast.

With our packs on our backs and a smile on our faces, we followed Kelly outside to her vehicle. We were in luck. Kelly is driving a Chevy Tahoe SUV. There will definitely be enough room to stretch our legs out. Kelly opened the rear hatch and said, "Throw your packs back here and grab a seat you two." We throw our packs in the back and Sam quickly jumped up front. Again, I was happy he did so as I noticed that back seat was more than big enough to accommodate a short nap along the way.

"Buckle up!" Kelly stated as we started off down the road. I thought, now would be a great time to get to know Kelly. "Where are you from Kelly?" I asked. "I'm originally from Pocatello, Idaho, but I've been living in Boise for the past five years," Kelly replied. "You are a long way from home, what brings you here?" Sam asked. "I'm on my way to visit some friends that live in the Dakotas," Kelly replied.

Kelly was just as curious to get to know the both of us. "Where are you two from?" Kelly asked. "We are from Spokane, Washington," Sam replied. "I've been to Spokane before, I really liked it there," Kelly stated. "Well, why are you two so far away as well?" She added. "After living in Spokane all our lives, we decided it was time to see what the rest of the country has to offer. You know, see if the grass is greener on the other side." I answered. "I totally understand. I kind of do the same thing, except I return to my home in Boise after each trip," Kelly replied.

"We don't have a home to return to. We are both just winging it out here," I added. "It would be nice to have a home to go to when we are done, but we don't have that right now," Sam replied. "What happened to the home you left in Spokane?" Kelly asked. "Well, it's a very long story. My mom passed away recently and the home we were staying in wasn't exactly hers, so we had to leave with nowhere to go. That's when we decided to go on this journey. I guess I am trying to find my calling and Sam is just along for the crazy ride." I replied.

"So, you both have no plan or direction you are going in. You're just winging it. That's very brave of you both. I know I could never do something like that without knowing where I'm going or how I'm getting there," Kelly replied. "That's what this adventure is all about. To see what we can do and where we may end up at," I stated. "Well, sit back and enjoy the ride. I've got the wheel, you two just relax." Kelly exclaimed.

After an hour of driving, Sam and I begin to become a little drowsy. Being a passenger in a vehicle has the same effect that parents do with young children when attempting to get them to sleep. Sam had placed his seat back in the reclining position and closed his eyes. I kept an eye on Kelly for a moment, trying to see if it was safe to take a nap. Keep in mind, we just met her and we know nothing about her. Of course, I trusted Mountain Flower to make the right decision when choosing a driver for us.

I started to close my eyes, not paying any attention to the highway signs as we drove on. My trust was in Kelly to get us where we need to go. The back seat of the Chevy Tahoe was comfortable enough to fall into a deep sleep. Pretty soon, I was out like a light.

Suddenly I woke up as if it was only fifteen minutes. To my surprise, it was One O'clock in the afternoon. "Good Afternoon sleepyhead," Kelly stated. "Where are we?" I asked. "I'm just about to pull over into a rest stop to use the restroom. You guys should get out and stretch your legs, you've been sleeping for a while." Kelly replied. I looked out the window to see we are at mile marker 168 as the rest stop was fast approaching.

I shook Sam's shoulder to wake him up. "Sam, we are at a rest stop, get out and use the restroom buddy" I exclaimed. We pulled off the highway into the rest stop parking. Kelly found a parking spot right by the front of the rest stop. We all got out of the vehicle to stretch our legs. Our legs felt so stiff from being in the vehicle so long. "I'm heading to the restroom" Kelly stated. Sam walked to the men's room as I wandered to the information board to find out exactly where we are.

As I am reading the information board, I see in big letters, Bismarck, North Dakota. Wait a minute, why are we in Bismarck, North Dakota. Why are we not in South Dakota? I ran towards the restroom as Sam is coming towards me. "Sam, you will not believe it dude, but we are in Bismarck, North Dakota" I frantically told him. Sam replied, "So, what's the big deal." With a dumbfounded look on my face, I replied, "We are supposed to be in South Dakota, not North Dakota! I thought Kelly knew where we are going!"

We're both freaking out as Kelly is coming towards us. "Are you guys ok?" Kelly asked. "Well, we are ok and we are not ok. Did Mountain Flower tell you where exactly we are trying to go to?" "She just said you were headed east with no particular destination in mind. But I'm getting the hint that we may not be where you thought you were going to be.

"It's ok, it's not anyone's fault. I guess I wasn't clear on where Sam and I are headed" I replied. "So where are you two trying to get too?" Kelly asked. "We wanted to go to Mount Rushmore in South Dakota" I advised. "Oh no, I'm sorry guys, but I am headed to Fargo, North Dakota. We are on Interstate 94 not Interstate 90. It's ok though, once we get to Fargo, we may arrange a ride to Mount Rushmore" Kelly stated.

Sam and I quickly talked and realized that we are not really on a time schedule and this mishap it actually alright. It is an opportunity to see a part of the country that we have not seen before. Plus, how bad can Fargo be right? I turned to Kelly and said, "It's alright Kelly, you didn't know and I didn't communicate our direction very well. We will be just fine traveling to Fargo with you."

I ran in to use the restroom while Sam and Kelly returned to her vehicle. Even though we have smoothed out our issue, I have anxiety about where we are and where we are going. I have heard little about Fargo, but I'm sure it should be an alright place to hang out for a moment. I finished using the restroom and headed to Kelly's SUV to continue our journey. This time I am keeping my eyes peeled to make sure we are going in the right direction.

We are just about three hours from Fargo, so it won't be a terrible ride. I have noticed the scenery is turning to a rural setting and not so much urban. Sam really wasn't affected by the miscommunication in directions. He's up for anything, I guess. I'm sure my anxiety will go away soon. Now I'm curious to see what's in Fargo. We made it through Montana, so Fargo, North Dakota couldn't possibly be any worse or desolate.

North Dakota is just about the same as Montana as far as roadkill goes. Poor dead animals all along the interstate. Kelly was good and able to drive around the slaughtered mess. She didn't want to get any blood on her tires or vehicle. I did notice a lot of dead porcupines along with small dear. It's really too bad that the animals have to die in this manner. I always say that the animals were here first and we as humans are invading their space and constructing roads through their homes.

After a few hours we were finally getting to Kelly's final stop in Fargo, North Dakota. I was looking all around for tall buildings or any sign of a bustling city. To my dismay, Fargo was just another small town. There was really nothing to be desired. I'm pretty sure I could walk from one end of town to the other in thirty minutes. I could be wrong, but I'm going to say that Fargo, North Dakota is the most boring town in the United States.

"Are you guys hungry" Kelly asked. We both nodded yes with empty bellies on our mind. We have good in our packs, but it's always better when somebody else cooks for you. Within minutes, we were pulling over and parking at a meter in the middle of downtown. I looked up to see a sign that read "The Old Broadway." It appeared to be your typical small downtown diner.

We all got out of Kelly's vehicle and headed in to grab a seat. As soon as we walked in, it was like a record player skipping a beat. Everybody in the diner turned and looked at us as if they knew we were not from there. We sat down at a table as our server brought us water and menus. I didn't need the menu since I always get the same thing. I ordered my country fried steak and eggs from the menu. Kelly and Sam ordered the pancakes and eggs. Sam can put down at least six pancakes before his gut explodes.

It wasn't too long before our server named June, was bringing out our food. I saw the cook in the kitchen. He was your typical short-order cook as if he was straight out of the movies. The portions were so big that I knew I could not finish my plate. We scarfed down as much as possible before paying our bill and leaving.

We still had a mini crisis on our hands as we needed to figure out how to get to Mount Rushmore in South Dakota. Kelly began calling her friends in Fargo hoping anybody could give us a ride. The one thing we didn't realize is Mount Rushmore is eight hours away. Getting anyone to commit to that drive is proving more difficult. We got lucky when we met Kelly. She was the right person at the right time.

Chapter 6

A Greyhound Adventure

It's starting to get dark as we ponder our options. Suddenly Kelly chimed in, "Wait a minute, the Greyhound Bus Station is two blocks away. It would cost you thirty dollars each to ride the bus to Mount Rushmore." I couldn't believe it. Why did we not think of this before? Sam and I have plenty of money for the tickets and that would solve our problem. "Let's do it!" Sam replied. I was in total agreement.

Kelly gave us one last ride over to the Greyhound Station. We grabbed our packs as we were saying goodbye. "Here is my number if you two are ever in town again"

Kelly stated. It's highly doubtful, but I took her phone number, anyway. Sam and I said our final goodbye to Kelly as we walked into the station to purchase our tickets.

We walked up to the ticket counter with money in hand. We thankfully got our tickets to Mount Rushmore quickly as the bus was just pulling in. Sam and I only had to wait fifteen minutes before we boarded the bus. The driver took our luggage and placed it in the bottom cargo area as we searched for a place to sit. Luckily the seat at the back was open. I liked that seat because it was bigger than the rest of the seats, which is what Sam and I needed. It appears this bus ride was going to be just as boring as the city we are leaving.

It is a long ride to Mount Rushmore, so we settled into our seats to relax. We expected to have a nice quiet drive, but we were very wrong about that. About half way up the isle on the right was an older man who appeared to be heavily intoxicated by alcohol. He was causing a scene with the surrounding passengers. The driver had already warned him to stay in his seat and to stop bothering people.

I kept my eye on him for a couple hours, hoping he doesn't cause any problems with Sam, myself and everybody else. I thought just maybe he would calm down, but I was wrong. He continued to drink his alcohol as he became more unruly. This time he was getting up and out of his seat several times, bothering the other passengers.

An off-duty police officer was on the bus, but she could not do anything because it wasn't her jurisdiction. The only thing she could to is to make him get back in his seat and stop bothering people. We had hoped this would last the rest of the ride, but we were wrong. This went on for about four hours and it was getting tiring.

Fate finally took care of our issue when the drunk passenger walked up to the front of the bus. He was so drunk and could barely walk or stand that he kept falling onto other passengers on the bus. As the man made his way to the front of the bus, the bus driver told him repeatedly to sit back in his seat. The man did not listen though.

Unable to speak legibly, the intoxicated man spun around and fell backwards through the protective fiberglass door that separated the driver from the rest of the passengers. The man crashed right onto the ground and fell down the stairs at the front of the bus. The driver was finally fed up and called the State Patrol. We waited about fifteen minutes for them to arrive and finally arrest the man.

All because he wanted to be a drunk nuisance, now he gets to spend the weekend in jail. After the arrest, the driver got back onto the bus and continued on to our destination. Everybody cheered with excitement that the drunk man was gone. Sam and I were thankful. We went back to relaxing and looking out the window.

Unfortunately, this was not the end of our unruly passengers. There was a man and woman traveling together who were obviously on heroin. The couple kept getting out of their seats and stumbling towards the bathroom at the back of the bus. We knew it was bad when they were falling asleep on the way back to their seats.

The woman was falling on customers so much that one man had to physically escort her back to her seat. I'm not stupid, I know which drugs a person is on. I had nineteen years to get to know it by watching my mom and her friends. Luckily, the man and woman both fell asleep back in their seats for the remainder of the ride.

I tried really hard to enjoy the bus ride to Mount Rushmore, but in reality, the Greyhound bus was like a porta-potty on wheels. It smelled badly and was filled with some pretty crazy people of which some did not care too much about their own hygiene. I guess it could be worse in many ways. At least I had Sam to keep me company when we were not sleeping.

After taking a nap for a few hours, I noticed we were just pulling into the Greyhound Station in Bismarck, North Dakota. This was one of our stops to let people off and pick up more passengers. Sam asked, "How much farther do we have to go until we get to Mount Rushmore?" "We have a few more hours to go. I'm wide awake myself. Are you going to stay awake until we get there?" I replied. "I'll probably stay awake for the rest of the ride" Sam stated.

We waited at the Greyhound station as some people left and new people got on the bus. We had about fifteen minutes before we left. I turned to Sam, "Hey bro, do you want to step outside for a quick joint?" Sam replied, "Heck Yes! That will make the rest of the ride even better to tolerate." We both got up out of our seats to head to the front of the bus. We left our coats on the seat to ensure that nobody took our spot.

It was easier for us to stand with all the cigarette smokers in order to blend in. I fired up a joint inconspicuously turning away from the bus as not to show what we are smoking. One lady we were standing next to picked up on the smell of marijuana. She turned to us laughing and said, "It's pretty obvious what you two are smoking. Can I have a hit of that?" "Absolutely!" Sam replied. We are happy to share our smoke as long as nobody snitched on us.

The middle-aged women took a healthy hit and immediately began coughing. Sam and I laughed so hard because we were pretty much sufficiently stoned. It's nice to have a calm feeling on a somewhat stressful bus ride. The lady passed the joint back to me and said, "Thank you guys! That was exactly what I needed to tolerate this trip." "We are happy to oblige!" I replied. Sam and I finished the joint and got back on the bus. We knew very well if we got caught, we could be kicked off the bus, but that was the chance we will take.

Sam and I settled back into our seats and got comfortable for the remaining few hours of the trip to Mount Rushmore. We both put our headphones on to listen to some music. Our selection of music ranged from Alternative and Classic Rock to Country music. It was a mixed bag of tunes.

We zoned out on the music and scenery as we headed towards South Dakota. The closer we got the happier we became. I had never been to Mount Rushmore before, so that made it even better. I felt like a kid in a candy store.

I looked around the bus at the different people. I didn't want to talk to any of them, but at the same time, I tried to predict their situation and lifestyle just by looking at them. Some looked sad, some looked happy. Others were trying to keep their kids in check and most were listening to music just like Sam and I. The lonely driver at the front of the bus looked and acted like a Drill Sargent. He was rough in nature, not taking any crap from the passengers. He definitely stood his ground when dealing with the people.

I returned to focusing on my music. My MP3 player was filled with Three Doors Down and Nickelback. I totally understand those bands aren't for everyone, but I seemed to like them. I remember seeing Nickelback in concert with Creed and Sevendust at the Spokane Arena. I truly feel these bands fit my personality. They were easy going and sounded great.

It wasn't too long before Sam fell back asleep. He gets bored really easy and because of that he falls asleep just about anywhere he is. I stayed awake by looking out the windows at the scenery. I noticed as we got closer to South Dakota, the scenery was changing to include more trees and greenery. Compared to North Dakota's wheat fields and farms, South Dakota was looking to be a beautiful place.

Before too long we were pulling into the Greyhound Station in Rapid City, South Dakota. That was as far as we could go by bus to get to Mount Rushmore. Sam and I got off the bus and retrieved our packs from under the bus. We realized there is still a thirty-minute drive to Mount Rushmore from Rapid City. Our only choice was to hitchhike the rest of the way.

We are on highway sixteen, which is a well-traveled rode, so our chances of being picked up is pretty good. The road was wide with plenty of room for Sam and I to walk along the side. We kept an eye out for police due to the fact that hitchhiking is illegal around the country. There was no choice but to hitchhike. A cab ride would have been way too much money for a thirty-minute ride.

It didn't take long for somebody to pull off the highway in front of us. Sam and I approached the older truck to find a man inside. He appeared to be in his fifties, with slight grey hair and glasses. "Do you fellas need a ride?" The man asked. "We sure do" I replied. "Where are you two headed?" he asked. "We are headed to Mount Rushmore" I replied. "Well hop in, I would be happy to give you two a ride there" The man stated.

Sam and I hopped in the truck's cab. It was an older truck, so it didn't have a king cab. All three of us had to sit up front next to each other. We took off down the road to our destination. "My name is Henry. What are your names?" the man asked. "My name is Kyler, and this is Sam" I replied. "It's nice to meet you both" Henry stated. "It's nice to meet you also" Sam replied.

There was something odd about Henry. He seemed to take a big interest in the both of us. There was something creepy about him. Henry kept staring at us both. I knew that look from my past. Henry was possibly trying to pick up on Sam and I. We both kept our eye on him. I was sitting next to the passenger door, so Sam had to sit next to Henry. This really made Sam uncomfortable. I could see it in his eyes. Even though we are getting a ride from the older man, it would not be worth it if he is a creeper.

We had been driving for about fifteen minutes when Henry said, "Hey boys, I have something to show you." He reached for the glove box. As soon as I saw his hand getting close to us, I slammed my foot onto the glove box. I didn't know what was in there, but I could only image it would be some weapon. "No thank you!" I exclaimed. "I think this is a suitable spot to pull over and get out" Sam replied.

Henry was taken back by our actions. He knew he was going to have trouble from us if he opened that glove box. "Please pull over!" I asked. "Ok, no problem!" Henry replied as he pulled over to the side of the road. "You are still about ten minutes from Mount Rushmore. I would be happy to give you a ride the rest of the way." Henry said. "That's ok, we can walk from here" I replied.

Sam and I got out of the truck and grabbed our packs. We thanked Henry for the ride as he pulled away back to the highway. "It's only a couple miles away" I said. "We can do it. It's better than taking a chance with that creepy guy" Sam replied. We put our packs on our backs and continued toward Mount Rushmore. It wouldn't be too long before we reach our destination.

After walking for about twenty minutes we finally saw the faces of Mount Rushmore. It became clearer as we got closer. Sam and I decided we didn't need to go right up to the mountain. We stopped in front of the Café that was near the parking lot. Mount Rushmore was very clear to the point we didn't need to take the trail right up to it. Plus, we wanted to get something to eat at the Café.

In 1923 Doane Robinson came up with the idea for Mount Rushmore to promote tourism in South Dakota. In 1924, Robinson had sculptor Gutzon Borglum travel to the Black Hills to ensure the carving could be started and finished.

The mountain turned into a massive sculpture carved into Mount Rushmore in the Black Hills region of South Dakota. It was completed in 1941 under the direction of Gutzon Borglum and his son Lincoln, the sculpture's roughly 60-ft.-high granite faces depict U.S. presidents George Washington, Thomas Jefferson, Theodore Roosevelt and Abraham Lincoln.

Sam and I were in awe of Mount Rushmore. We had seen nothing like it before. I couldn't believe that a group of men could carve such a huge piece of art into the side of a mountain. I took pictures with a Kodak disposable camera. I didn't want to forget this moment.

I wasn't happy to find out the actual history of Mount Rushmore and how the land was taken by the U.S. Government. To many Native Americans, Mount Rushmore represents a desecration of lands considered sacred by the Lakota Sioux, the original residents of the Black Hills region who were displaced by white settlers and gold miners in the late nineteenth century.

In the Treaty of Fort Laramie, signed in 1868 by Sioux tribes and General William T. Sherman, the U.S. government promised the Sioux "undisturbed use and occupation" of territory including the Black Hills, in what is now South Dakota. But the discovery of gold in the region soon led U.S. prospectors to flock there, and the U.S. government began forcing the Sioux to relinquish their claims on the Black Hills.

Warriors like Sitting Bull and Crazy Horse led a concerted Sioux resistance (including the latter's famous defeat of Gen. George Armstrong Custer in the Battle of the Little Bighorn in 1876), which federal troops eventually crushed in a brutal massacre at Wounded Knee in 1890. Ever since then, Sioux activists have protested the U.S. confiscation of their ancestral lands, and demanded their return. The Black Hills are important to them, as the region is central to many Sioux religious traditions.

We took as many pictures as possible and stood in awe before entering the café to eat some dinner. "This is it. The entire reason for coming here. Here we are at the base of Mount Rushmore. I will never forget this moment" I said to Sam. It wouldn't be too long before finished and headed out to find a place to camp overnight in Custer National Park. We were very discrete about what we were doing. Though we didn't enter through the main trails like everybody else. Sam and I found our way through the trees and bushes to find the perfect place to sleep under the stars.

There was no need to set up any tents in this area. The temperature was around 70 degrees, which made it easier to fall asleep. We will continue our journey in the morning. "Good night Sam" I said to Sam. "Good night Kyler" Sam replied.

Chapter 7

The Mile-High Conspiracy

Sam and I woke from a wonderful night's sleep. Nobody found us sleeping in the park which enabled us to sleep all the way through the night. I took the single burner butane stove out of my backpack and prepared to make some oatmeal for the both of us. Sam loved oatmeal of any kind. I am ok with it, but it's not my favorite.

We are preparing for our next adventure down the road. "Where do you want to go next?" I asked Sam. "We can go anywhere, but I'm not sure on where we should go. There are so many choices. Where do you want to go?" Sam replied. "I kind of want to go to Denver, Colorado. I've studied the controversies surrounding the Denver International Airport and I've always wanted to go there in person to see all the things I have studied," I replied.

"That sounds great to me. I've also always wanted to go see what everybody is talking about. It was be so awesome if we could make our way underground, if you know what I mean," Sam replied. "That settles it then, we are on our way to the Denver International Airport. It's almost 6 hours away driving, so we better get our stuff together and see if we can hitch a ride with somebody," I replied.

We quickly ate our oatmeal breakfast and packed up all of our gear. The coast was clear to make our way out of the park before it opened back up to the public. Sam and I were back on the highway with our thumbs out desperately looking for a ride towards Denver, Colorado.

It wasn't too long before we were picked up by a nice older couple in an SUV, heading south down the highway. The couple were driving to the Hot Springs just south of Wind Cave National Park. It wasn't too far, but it was worth the trip to get us a bit farther south.

The time went by quickly as we arrived at the Hot Springs quickly. "This is as far as we go, but we wish you luck" The older gentlemen said. "Thank you both for giving us a ride this far. We will continue on our way south" I replied. Sam and I retrieved our packs from the back of the SUV and continued our quest.

We noticed a few big rigs parked at the Hot Springs. There were three truckers that had stopped to enjoy the Hot Springs on their break from their route. "I wonder if we can get one trucker to give us a ride farther south" I stated. "Let's stand by the trucks and wait for them to return. It doesn't hurt to ask each one" Sam replied.

Sam couldn't have spoken too soon as one of the truckers came along to get into his truck. I ran up to him and said, "Excuse me sir, my friend and I are trying to go south towards the Denver International Airport and we were wondering if you give us a ride." The driver quickly replied, "I apologize guys, but I am driving north to Wisconsin. I know of one driver that is headed for Denver. As a matter of fact, here he comes now."

We looked over and saw a big man coming our way. He was your typical truck driver, large and gruff looking. I waited for him to reach us when I asked, "Excuse me sir, my friend and I are attempting to go to the Denver International Airport and we heard you are going that way. We are wondering if you wouldn't mind letting us hitch a ride with you." The man replied, "Are you guys crazy?" Sam and I looked at each other with a blank look on our face.

The man said again, "Well, are you guys crazy or normal?" "We're normal, we're normal, I promise we are not crazy," I replied. "Ok then, jump in the passenger seat and let's go," the man stated. Sam and I were elated. "How far towards Denver are you going?" Sam asked. "I'm headed to the Shell Truck Stop, just about 5 miles south of the Denver International Airport. I can take you to the truck stop or I can drop you off right outside the airport," the man replied.

"We'll take the offer of dropping us off right outside the airport. Thank you so much, we really appreciate this. We are kind of on a journey of sorts," I said. "My name is Big Bart. What are your names?" Big Bart asked. "My name is Kyler, and this is my friend Sam. We are from Washington State," I replied. "What are you doing so far from home?" Big Bart asked. "Well, we are taking a trip across this great nation to see what adventure we can experience.

"Your hitchhiking across the country?" Bart asked. "I know it sounds crazy, but we are doing our best. So far, so good." I replied. "Well let's hit the road" Bart exclaimed. Before we knew it, we were on our way south down the highway. We are a few hours away from our destination. I couldn't believe we have hitchhiked a ride from a truck driver named Big Bart. This experience is priceless.

Sam and I minded our manners while inside Bart's truck. We could tell the truck was his only home. He had everything except the kitchen sink inside his truck. It was a good time to relax and enjoy the right while we are not on our feet.

We chatted with Big Bart the entire way. It kept us awake, and it kept Bart entertained. You could tell it has been a while since he had anybody inside his truck but himself. He seemed to enjoy himself. Before we knew it, the few hours had gone by quickly. We could see the teepee shaped structures in sight. That is the Denver International Airport. One of the most awesome looking airports in the entire country.

Finally, we made it to our destination. Big Bart pulled over to let us out. "You boys take care now, you hear," Bart said. "Thank you again for the ride, I wish there was some way to repay you," I replied. "Don't worry boys, it was fun and adventurous for me. So long gentlemen," Bart replied. We closed the door and sent Big Bart on his way.

We have made it to the Denver International Airport. We had about 6 blocks to walk before we were actually on the airport property. Sam and I quickly made our way to the main entrance. The Airport itself is humongous. It's an exquisite but intimidating airport. So much to see in the time you are here.

Sam and I are here for a different reason. We are not flying anywhere. Our plan is to investigate the entire airport. There is so many conspiracies surround the airport. Denver International Airport (DIA) has some secrets. At least, that's what conspiracy theorists on the internet will tell you.

Built as a replacement for Stapleton Airport, near Denver, in 1995, DIA has always had its share of nefarious conspiracy theories about it. From the beginning, Coloradoans have theorized about the airport's secret tunnels, clues to Nazi secret societies, and horrifying harbingers of doom "hidden" in public artwork around the Denver hub.

There are many theories about who built the Denver airport. One of the most persistent theories is that the airport was built by the New World Order with ties to

Nazism. The theory even goes so far as to say that the airport's runways are built to resemble a swastika from above. However, looking at photographs of their configuration, the runways don't seem to resemble that shape in particular unless you're really looking for it.

It doesn't help that the airport's dedication marker credits an organization called The New World Airport Commission for building it. This may seem like a coincidence, but it was discovered that such an organization doesn't exist.

People have also noted "strange" markings on buildings, which are believed to be connected with the New World Order, as well. In reality, many "mysterious" buildings markings are referencing the Navajo language or periodic table of elements. Still, it seems a little suspicious, right?

The Blue Mustang, also known as Blucifer, is a 32-foot fiberglass sculpture by artist Luis Jiménez, located along Peña Boulevard. It's inspired by the sculpture Mesteño, at the University of Oklahoma, but sinister events surrounding the sculpture have fueled conspiracy theories for years.

For one, people point to the statues glowing red eyes as a nod to the Four Horsemen of the Apocalypse, though the artist once said that the red color was in honor of the "wild" spirit of the American West. Sure, a likely story.

It doesn't help that Jiménez died two years before the piece was completed when a piece of the statue fell on him and severed an artery in his leg. Since then, people have been concocting all sorts of wild theories about the horse's purpose. As mundane as it is, it seems the horse is artwork, and nothing more.

Besides being built by some Nazi New World Order, rumors abound about the many unmarked buildings and underground areas on the airport's property. This theory may have stemmed from a time capsule buried on the property, which bears symbols from the Free Masons, which are "linked" to the Illuminati.

One of the main reasons this conspiracy theory has so much staying power is because the airport was much more expensive than originally projected. So, how was the airport completed? Conspiracy theorists point to Illuminati money, which some believe was used to finish DIA's construction in exchange for the secret society using the property.

Rumors say that the first few buildings on the property were not built properly, but instead of demolishing them, the airport buried them and built more buildings on top, giving the Illuminati its own "underground lair."

Rumors surrounding the apocalypse are probably some of the biggest conspiracy theories about the airport. Yes, there are underground tunnels in the airport, including a train that runs between concourses and a defunct automated baggage system. But the true nature of the tunnels is believed to be more nefarious.

Some have theorized that the tunnels also contain underground bunkers possibly built by Lizard People or aliens that will serve as a safe place for the world's elite during the apocalypse. Other theories say that the tunnels directly lead to the North American Aerospace Defense Command (NORAD), which is located only about 100 miles south of the airport, in Colorado Springs. However, it seems like an expensive mode of travel. Not to mention, the new DIA has only been open for about 25 years, and it could take decades to construct a tunnel of that length.

There are a lot of weird pieces of art throughout DIA as part of the airport's public art collection — besides the giant horse statue on Peña Boulevard. Some of these eerie artworks included murals by artist Leo Tanguma, which some believe have alleged Nazi imagery in the murals as proof that the airport is somehow linked to a fascist secret society.

In reality, Tanguma's murals are about world peace and a healthy environment. Though we can admit, the murals are pretty terrifying to look at despite their hopeful messages. Others are fixated on the random gargoyle statues that seem to watch over the airport.

While the gargoyles may seem a little suspicious, gargoyles have been used throughout the centuries in architecture as a totem to "ward off" evil spirits and protect the buildings. Many of the gargoyles are placed at baggage claim to protect traveler's luggage.

These are all conspiracy theories that Sam and I are going to investigate while we are at the Denver International Airport. Where do we begin and where do we end? We have to complete these investigations before the end of the day. We certainly cannot sleep overnight inside the airport. We must do quick investigations, then make our way outside to find a place to sleep overnight.

This is a once in a lifetime event for Sam and I. So many cool things to see in this enormous airport. I thought to myself, "There is no way we can cover everything. The airport is about fifty-six square miles of conspiracy. We will absolutely do our best to get some answers to our adventure."

It took us around six hours to cover the airport's conspiracies. I'm still baffled to this day that these clues are still inside the airport. Is it all true or is the airport feeding into the theories and making the airport a destination site for so many adventure seekers? We probably will never know the true answer to these things.

Sam and I had our fill of adventure today. Our feet are hurting and we desperately need to make something to eat and get some rest. Luckily, we are only a few miles from the Rocky Mountain Arsenal National Wildlife Refuge. This would be a perfect place to rest overnight. We had decided to get something to eat from one of the many fast-food places inside the airport. Sam and I just didn't have it in us to set up the cooker and make something to eat outside. Plus, we didn't want to attract the attention to any of the wildlife out there.

After eating a hearty meal at Burger King inside the airport, we made our way to an entrance until we were outside. The weather was glorious, and we had just a bit more energy to make it to the wildlife refuge to set up camp. "Are you still have a blast Sam?" I asked. "You better believe I am. Thank you for asking me to go on this adventure with you Kyler. I'm having the time of my life.

We made it to the wildlife refuge faster than we thought it would take. Sam and I are being incredibly careful to not disturb the area of the animals living in the refuge. I didn't see any warning signs about any particular animal that we should be aware of.

After walking a short distance from the main road, we could find the right spot to camp. It was just inside the line of trees and bushes, which is perfect for hiding from anyone on the road. Plus, there are no workers or Park Rangers around to kick us out. They probably don't get many people camping inside the refuge. We settled in for the night as we anticipate our next adventure. We are not sure where to go next, but wherever it is, we will make the best of it.

Chapter 8

You Turkey

The morning came quickly this time. We woke up to the sound of passing vehicles traveling up and down the highway. Luckily, we still haven't been bothered by anybody while sleeping under the stars. It is time to get our things together and continue on with our journey.

"Where are we going next Kyler?" Sam asked. "How about we check out the mid-west since we are in the area," I replied. "There is so much to see and experience," I added. "Alright, sounds good, but which direction should we choose?" Sam asked. "That's a good question Sam. Which direction should we choose?" I asked.

"Let's finish getting our stuff packed up and hit the road. We can decide the direction by who picks us up on the road" Sam replied. "Let's do it!" I exclaimed. It only took us a few more minutes to put all of our sleeping gear in our packs. We are ready to continue on with our journey. "Alright, let's hit the road Sam" I said.

We made our way out of the brush and up to the road. We started walking east with our thumbs out, hoping for anybody to pick us up. It was taking a minute this time. Vehicle after vehicle was passing us by. We are ok with this for now, because we knew already that this may happen. Not everyone trusts a hitchhiker in this day and age.

Just as we thought we would never get picked up; a king cab Chevy truck pulled off the highway in our direction. We saw a hand reach out the window and wave out the driver's side window, motioning us to come forward. Sam and I must be the luckiest hitchhikers on the road.

It only took us about five seconds to reach the truck. I went around to the driver's side to discover a middle-aged man with a grey beard sitting there waiting for us to arrive. I asked the man, "Which direction are you headed?" He replied, "Get in the truck and we will discuss it. I have a job opportunity for you."

Sam and I walked around to the passenger side of the truck and opened the door. Sam jumped in first, making his way to the back of the king cab. I hopped into the passenger seat up front. "So, what are you men doing out on the road?" the man asked. "We are out here for the unknown adventures. My name is Kyler, and this is Sam. What's your name?" I asked. "My name is Tom; most people call me Turkey Tom" the man replied.

"Why do they call you that?" Sam asked. "Well, I own a turkey farm in Aurora, Nebraska. I saw the both of you and felt that you seemed to be two strong men that wouldn't mind making some money on my farm. It would be definitely worth your while. I would happily pay you each $800 per week, plus room and board." Tom replied.

"We know nothing about turkeys, except eating them," I stated. "Don't worry about any experience. I will train you both and you will be just fine." Tom replied. I looked back at Sam and said, "What do you think Sam?" "I'm up for it. Why not give it a try!" Sam replied. I turned to Tom, "Alright sir, you have two hard workers that would like to join your team for the season. By the way, how long is the season?" I asked.

"The turkey raising season is about four months until the end of September when the turkeys are taken away by the butcher for the holiday season," Tom added. "That would be great. We can earn some money that will help us on our way around the country," I added. "So, what is Aurora like," Sam asked.

"Well, Aurora is in Hamilton County, but filled with mostly corn fields. Our population is roughly four thousand people, most of whom are farmers. Our claim to fame is that the inventor of the strobe light is from Aurora. That's about the only famous thing we have going. There is much to explore within the community, as well as throughout the surrounding Hamilton County area. You may not take in all the incredible experiences Aurora has to offer in just one trip, so fair warning; you might need to plan a follow-up visit."

"While you're in Aurora, don't pass up the chance to stroll around Central Park Square, informally known as 'The Square.' The beautifully preserved courthouse, inviting lawn, and historic shops truly make this a one-of-a-kind destination in Nebraska. I will be more than happy to give you both a tour of the town once we get you both settled in.

If we make a day trip during the summer months, we will be trying homegrown and homemade goods. The farmer's market includes, but is not limited to, fresh vegetables, pastries, and home-canned goods. The market is first-come, first-served, so we have to arrive early to select the best produce and homemade treats.

Each summer harvests a new, unique mixture of vendors and goodies. What makes our market special are the vendors themselves. Each has a story about why they are there. Our vendors have joined for reasons that involve desiring a second income, wanting a hobby, needing a fund for college, and hoping to save the environment. Regardless of what draws our vendors to the farmer's market, they are continuously a joyful bunch."

"We'll get to all of that when we have time. For now, strap on your seatbelts. We should arrive in Aurora in about five hours. We'll stop every so often to stretch our legs and use the rest stop restrooms. Do you two have any questions?" Tom asked. "I think you covered everything Tom. We are honored to be along for the ride and assist you on your farm." I replied.

After a long drive, we finally made our way to Aurora, Nebraska. The weather was perfect and the view of the corn fields are very peaceful. It wouldn't be long before we arrive at Tom's turkey farm. Sam and I are looking forward to this adventure. Neither of us have ever experienced working at a real farm.

We arrive at the gate to the farm, just under a sign that read "Norbest Turkeys". I've had these turkeys before, but had no idea that Tom is the owner of this one farm. Norbest is a household name when it comes to turkeys. I can't believe this is the farm we get to work on for the next four months.

After arriving at Tom's home, we were treated to a big lunch that Tom's wife Jenny had made for us. There was potato salad and a huge spread of sandwiches. It was a build your own sandwich type of meal. Sam and I loaded up on ham, chicken and of course, turkey on our sandwiches. There was enough fresh vegetable to compete with a Subway sandwich shop.

We filled our bellies until we could eat no more. "Well boys, you are all fed. How about I show you the turkey farm? I'll show you around while Jenny is getting your room ready. We'll wait until tomorrow morning before we start your first day.

Sam and I got up from our seats and followed Tom outside. We could hear the turkeys gobbling, but we could not see them yet. There are corn fields as far as the eye could see. I felt like we were in the baseball movie "Field of Dreams", but there was no Kevin Costner to be found.

"Let's go check out the turkeys", Tom stated. "Alright we are excited to see all the turkeys", I replied. We rounded the corner to the turkey barns and suddenly the sheer amount of turkeys hit our eyes. "Wow, that is a ton of turkeys" I exclaimed. There are turkeys everywhere. Not just a few, but thousands. "How many turkeys do you have Tom?" Sam asked.

"Right now, you are looking at forty thousand full grown turkeys in those four barns. That's ten thousand per barn. I have another twenty thousand in the incubation barn." "This is no joke Tom", I exclaimed with excitement. "It's a little intimidating", Sam added. There are turkeys everywhere. Sam and I could not believe our eyes.

"Alright boys, your work starts tomorrow morning right after breakfast at 4:30 AM. Go ahead and explore the rest of the farm on your own. Try to get to know the place. Dinner is at 6:00 PM sharp, so don't be late," Tom replied.

It was still a beautiful day for exploring. The farm was picture perfect. The old barns and new barns mixed together showing the generations of work that took place on this farm. Sam and I wanted to see the turkeys for ourselves.

When we walked into the turkey barn, I was taken aback by how spacious it is. If you've ever walked onto a football field, have you noticed how long it is? The playing field is 100 yards, or 300 feet. This turkey house was twice that; it was 600 feet long. There was a lot of open space, yet the turkeys were all in the same general area. Turns out, turkeys are sociable birds and like to be around each other. Given the choice, they will stick together.

The turkeys gathered around us and moved as a group while we walked through the turkey barn. We walked through the middle of the flock which was like the parting of the Red Sea, but they soon gathered together again. Once they decided we weren't interesting anymore, they moved away and went back to doing turkey things.

This is definitely a new experience for Sam and I. This is a different way of life that we will never forget. We avoided the incubation barn until Tom was with us. I'm sure that something terrible could go wrong if we started snooping about.

After a long day of exploring the farm and corn fields, Sam and I made our way back to the main house for dinner. Of course, we are having turkey for dinner. Fresh from the farm. It's a team effort between Tom and Jenny. Tom would kill the turkey of choice and Jenny would pluck out all the feathers. The turkey we ate that night was tender and juicy just like if you would have purchased it from the grocery store.

Sam and I felt our bellies becoming fuller after each bite we took. I for one, felt like my stomach was about to explode. Tom and Jenny put out a big spread of food. This is what we get to look forward to every night.

After we ate, Sam and I took turns taking a shower. It had been such a long day and we are exhausted. "You boys get some sleep. We are early to rise in the morning. Be prepared to do some turkey work tomorrow. Sam and I went up to our room on the second floor. It was kind of like a worker's dorm with two beds per room. I have a feeling Tom has had seasonal workers here regularly. I guess we just got lucky this time around.

The next morning came quickly. Sam and I both awoke to the smell of breakfast. We quickly made our way downstairs to see what was cooking. Jenny had prepared a hearty meal. "Pull up a seat at the table boys. We have eggs, bacon, sausage, hash browns, country gravy and orange juice so dig in" Jenny said.

This had to have been the biggest breakfast we have had so far on our journey. Tom came in and joined us. "Are you men ready to work?" Tom asked. "We are ready and willing to learn", I replied. "Show us the ropes" Sam added.

"The first thing we need to do is look for Snipes," Tom mentioned. "What are Snipes?" I asked. "Snipes are little birds that bring disease to the turkeys. It could kill the entire farm," Tom responded. "Let's go outside and I will show you how to catch Snipes. I need you to both hold a black garbage bag with a flash light inside the bag. Then shake the bushes by the barn to find the Snipes. We'll collect them and end their life." Tom added.

Sam and I grabbed the black plastic garbage bags and one flashlight each. We quickly went to work trying to find the Snipes. We're shaking every bush in sight, but for some odd reason, we were not finding any Snipes to capture. "Are you sure they're here?" I asked Tom. "Just keep looking gentlemen. You'll find them." Tom replied.

We were searching and searching, shaking every bush possible in the morning darkness. Then all of a sudden Sam and I hear a fit of laughter in the background. It was Tom and Jenny. There were both laughing their asses off at us. I looked over at Sam and said, "I think we are part of one big joke. I don't believe there is any bird called a Snipe. I think we are looking for nothing."

Tom and Jenny realized that we have figured out their joke as they laughed harder and harder. "You've been initiated boys. Come on back. There is no such thing as Snipes!" Tom laughed. They continued laughing as Sam and I made our way back to the house. It was hilarious, they got us that morning. I was liking Tom and Jenny even more. I love their sense of humor.

Over the next four months Sam and I worked harder than we ever did before in our lives. It was a usual routine every morning. We would wake up at 4:30 AM and eat breakfast. Then our work routine took place. This never changed over the course of time we were there.

Our daily routing after breakfast would be to count the dead turkeys and throw them in the incinerator. Unfortunately, some turkeys died of suffocation. At night when the air is cold, the turkeys would all huddle together to keep themselves warm by piling on top of one another. This resulted in the death of some of the turkeys at the bottom. They would literally become flat as a pancake by morning time. The smell of the dead turkey's was horrible, but we had masks on to cover up some of the smell.

After taking care of the dead, we would then feed and water the rest of the turkeys. Sam and I never went into the incubation barn. That is something Tom and Jenny tended to on their own. There was one job that Sam and I never liked to do. We had to stick our finger up the turkey's butt in order to test them for E. coli. This was necessary to maintain their contract with Norbest Turkey and for the health and safety of the public.

Tom was always trying to get Sam and I to hit a turkey over the head with a baseball bat in order to have a turkey for dinner. We both declined that role and left it up to Tom to take care of. One of the best parts of working on the farm was when Tom would allow Sam and I to ride his stock car that he built. We would take it out on the muddy track. We also could drive Tom's Four-Wheelers and jump over piles of manure all over the farm.

It wasn't long before our time at the turkey farm was over. The four months have come and past. Our last duty on the farm was to help load the turkeys onto the semi-truck to send them off to be butchered at the end of September.

Sam and I figured our next adventure would be to head to the southern states as the weather became colder up north. We studied the U.S. map and decided on New Orleans, Louisiana. This would be a great destination because of the higher temperatures and humidity. It would make for some nice nights sleeping under the stars or wherever we may find ourselves.

Chapter 9

The Voodoo State

Tom gave us a ride to the nearest Greyhound Station at Love's Truck Stop in Aurora. We told Tom that Sam and I wanted to take the Greyhound bus since we made some good cash within the past 4 months. Tom had insisted on buying our tickets to New Orleans. It was only fifty dollars each so we allowed Tom to purchase the tickets.

We are very grateful for all that Tom and Jenny had done for us. Who knows where we would have been if Tom had not pulled over that day, last June?

An American Son: Kyler's Journey

Sam and I are getting used to routine on the Greyhound. It's still not a pleasant way to travel. It's convenient and inexpensive, but the hospitality is never there. I would truly recommend the Greyhound bus to someone that has no other choice to travel.

It took us about twenty hours of traveling before we made it to New Orleans, Louisiana. This is both our first time here. To me, New Orleans is filled with mystery and power. The Voodoo history, the above ground cemeteries and the vampire fantasy.

New Orleans is on the Mississippi River, near the Gulf of Mexico. Nicknamed the "Big Easy," it's known for its round-the-clock nightlife, vibrant live-music scene and spicy, singular cuisine reflecting its history as a melting pot of French, African and American cultures. Embodying its festive spirit is Mardi Gras, the late-winter carnival famed for raucous costumed parades and street parties.

Either way, we are excited to be here and are ready for some adventure. The only place to start our time here is at the French Quarter. The French Quarter is the city's historic heart, famous for its vibrant nightlife and colorful buildings with cast-iron balconies. Crowd-pleasing Bourbon Street features jazz clubs, Cajun eateries and raucous bars serving potent cocktails. Quieter streets lead to the French Market, with gourmet food and local crafts, and to Jackson Square where street performers entertain in front of soaring St. Louis Cathedral.

As we are making our way through Bourbon Street, Sam looks up at a sign on a building. I stopped to see what he was looking at. I could not believe my eyes. What was Sam thinking? We had stopped in front of a strip club. "Sam we are not going inside there, no way!" I exclaimed. "Oh, come on Kyler, it's our once in a lifetime experience. Sam replied.

I reluctantly agreed to go into the strip club. "You're paying for this Sam" I stated. With a huge grin on his face, Sam got some money out of his pockets and gave it to the door man. The door man asked, "Hey how about a tip for the door man" Sam and I looked at each other and I said, "Well give the man a tip." Sam reached in his pocket again and gave the door man five dollars as he let us in the strip club.

It was dark and mysterious inside the club. Half-naked women were everywhere. I couldn't believe what I was seeing. This is the very first time that I have stepped inside a club like this. The music was good, and the alcohol flowed freely.

I looked towards the stage and saw a shirtless young lady with no bra on. I'm pretty sure my face was redder than the carpet we were standing on. Sam was all smiles. If his smile could get any bigger, he could've played the Joker in a Batman movie.

Sam and I made our way to the stage and sat down to front row seats. Sam pulled out a stack of one-dollar bills as the young lady came over to us. She squatted down right in front of us, with her pelvic area right in our face.

I was so embarrassed. But not Sam, he started giving her dollar bill after dollar bill. The young lady stayed right in front of us until he had gone through all of his single dollars. As the lady walked to the stripper pole in the middle of the stage, Sam reached inside his pocket for more cash. "Let's get some drinks" Sam exclaimed. "Just one drink Sam, that is all" We both ordered a rum and coke. I figured; we must play the part if we are going to be inside this joint.

After spending fifty dollars in less than thirty minutes, I urged Sam to leave this place. "Sam, if we don't get up and leave right now, this place is going to get all of your money you've earned over the past four months. Let's get up and go now," I told Sam. "Fine, fine let's go I guess," Sam replied.

As we were leaving the strip club, Sam asked, "Where are we going now." I replied, "I want to go to a voodoo shop and buy a voodoo doll." We proceeded down Bourbon Street checking out every store we passed. The streets were full of people as it was standing room only. It kind of felt like I was at a carnival and the stores were filled with Carnies, just waiting to suck all the money out of a person.

Then we saw it. The one place I really wanted to go. It was Marie Laveau's House of Voodoo. I have wanted to come here ever since we mentioned we were coming to New Orleans. Marie Catherine Laveau was a Louisiana Creole practitioner of Voodoo, herbalist, and midwife who was renowned in New Orleans. Her daughter, Marie Laveau II, also practiced root work, conjure, Native American and African spiritualism as well as Louisiana Voodoo. Whether you're on a ghost tour, a voodoo tour, or a historical tour of New Orleans, the chances are high that you will hear stories and legends of the City's beloved Queen of Voodoo, Marie Laveau.

Marie Laveau was a free person of color living in the most colorful city in the United States, New Orleans. An article in The New Orleans Times Picayune, April 1886, adoringly remembered Marie Laveau, as "gifted with beauty and intelligence, she ruled her own race, and made captive of many of the other." A Creole woman with her own set of rules and strong beliefs who was surrounded by the political and religious influence of wealthy white men. Marie Laveau was a trailblazer for all women, her strong convictions and loyal confidentiality have kept her a mysterious legend for centuries.

I was hooked from the start. I'm into mysterious occupations and tales of magic. Sam and I immediately went inside the voodoo shop and viewed her goods for sale. I went right for the voodoo dolls. I really wanted to have one. I spoke to the cashier for a minute about the dolls. She asked me what kind of future I would like to have. I mentioned that I would like to be financially free and the one to take care of my family.

She immediately showed me the voodoo doll of money. It was brown with black hair and a penny over each eye. The kind lady advised me not to use it for evil but only for good. I promised to use the doll only for good purposes. I purchased the doll for fifteen dollars and quickly placed it in my backpack.

Sam wanted nothing from the store. He believed it would bring him bad luck if he purchased anything for himself. "Oh well, to each their own" I laughed. After completing my purchase, it was back to Bourbon Street for us. We were both hungry and ready to eat some dinner.

There was a nice restaurant that served your average bar food like nachos, tacos, hamburgers and fries. We stepped inside and grabbed a seat for the both of us. As we were sipping on our beer, waiting for our meal, I looked over to see who was sitting at the table next to us. The voice sounded familiar but I couldn't figure it out until I looked.

I couldn't believe it. Sam and I were having dinner, sitting right next to Bob Saget from Full House and Jonathan Silverman from the movie Weekend at Bernie's. I was in pure shock. I had never been that close to a celebrity before.

Bob Saget noticed I was staring, and he turned to Sam and I and said "Hello". All I could do is smile and say "Hello" back to them. What a weird world when you can innocently walk into a bar and see a famous person sitting there like it is normal for them. Sam and I made sure not to bug them again for the rest of the time at our table.

We were getting tired and decided to leave and find a hotel for the night. We had a lot of extra money. There was no reason to sleep outside that night. We paid out bill and said goodnight to Bob and Johnathan. They remained gracious to us both as we left.

The walk to the hotels was not too far. We had decided to stay at the Marriott downtown. It was about six blocks from Bourbon Street. The price was right, and the amenities were great. Another surprise was headed our way. As we were checking in, two men had just come in to check in.

Sam looked over, then looked at me with a surprised look. "Look who it is Kyler!" he exclaimed. I turned to my right to see Fats Domino and Smokey Robinson checking into the hotel. I couldn't believe it. How can one night be so great?

This was just too much for me. Sam and I got our room key and headed up to our fancy double room. It was a very nice room with two beds and a living room area to relax. We quickly settled in and cleaned ourselves up. After sitting there for an hour, we decided it was a good time to head to the hotel bar for a beer.

The craziest thing is the entire time we were in New Orleans, nobody ever checked our identification. If they did, they would have seen that we were only twenty years old. Oh well, it was fun crashing the party.

Chapter 10

Florida Bound

We woke up the next morning with huge headaches. We may have drunk a little too much while enjoying the festivities. After taking showers, Sam and I headed downstairs to the restaurant for breakfast. We have a couple hours before we have to check out, so it's time to fill our bellies.

After all the fun we had in New Orleans, we wanted to keep the fun times going. It took some time to ponder where we should be next. It had to be close, and it had to be full of adventure.

It took a while, but an idea popped into my head. We are close to Florida, which means we are close to my friends Hubert and Rella. They live in Clearwater, Florida, just outside of Tampa. I have always wanted to go to Florida and now is our chance.

Sam and I still had more than enough money between us. It was an easy decision to take a flight to Florida. Both of us are really trying to avoid the Greyhound bus for as long as possible. We had no interest in traveling inside of a porta-potty on wheels.

We finished our breakfast and felt it was a good time to get our things together and check out. First, I wanted to contact Hubert and Rella to make sure it was ok for us to go to Florida. I knew they would say yes, but I wanted to make sure.

It didn't take long for us to arrive at our room to pack our belongings. While Sam was completing the packing, I called Hubert from the hotel room. Hubert immediately said yes, they would be happy to have us at their home. I couldn't wait. Hubert was seriously excited to see us. I hadn't seen them in a few years, so this was going to be amazing.

I called Alaska Airlines and booked two tickets to Florida. It was literally less than two hours in the air before we would arrive. Our plane isn't leaving until 2:00 PM so we had a couple of hours to kill. "We should get to the airport and hour early, just to make sure we are safe and on time" Sam stated. "I agree, we could get there early to ensure we are on time." I replied.

An American Son: Kyler's Journey

We quickly grabbed our items and headed downstairs to the main floor. There were no shortage of taxi cabs sitting out front. It was nice to just hop in a cab without having to call and wait for one to arrive. We grabbed the first one in line. "To the airport please" I advised the driver.

The closer we got to the airport, the more excited Sam, and I became. This will be our first flight on our trip around the country. Who knows what fun and adventure we will find in Florida? I'm really curious what jobs we will obtain during our stay.

We are pretty much up for anything as far as the jobs go. Hubert and Rella will show us around the city. They warned us it is very hot in Florida, with high humidity all the time. Coming from the cold Pacific Northwest, both Sam and I are ready for some heat.

It wasn't too long before we reached the airport. The cab driver pulled up to the drop off spot right in front of the many entrances. I paid the driver as we exited the car to grab our packs out of the trunk of the cab. We are still one hour early, so we went in to get some Gatorade. After last night, we needed to reload on our electrolytes. Sometimes the alcohol can do a number on a person the next morning.

Sam and I entered the airport eager to find our way to our gate. There are so many shops we passed on the way; we could grab our drinks on the run. This airport is pretty nice. Everybody is so friendly here. That's the New Orleans hospitality everyone talks about. The people are very gracious.

We finally made our way to our gate and grabbed some seats right up front while we waited to board the airplane. There are so many people from all over the country in this airport right now. It's fascinating to be part of such a mix of people.

The hour went by when the desk agent got on the intercom and called out for our flight to Florida. We all stood up and got in line, ready to board the plane. "I can't wait to get to Florida", Sam stated. "Me too!" "This is going to so much fun. I can't wait to see Hubert and Rella," I replied.

We got to the front of the line and handed our boarding passes to the agent at the door. She scanned us right in and we took off down the walk way to the airplane. We were greeted by the pilot and flight attendants. Sam and I could get seats right next to each other. "I want the window seat" I told Sam. "No problem buddy, it's all yours" Sam replied.

We settled into our seats and prepared for take-off. This is only the second time that I've been on a plane. I still hold on to the seat arms when taking off, as if I will fly out of my seats. It sounds crazy, but I like it when the plane gets up to the highest speed before lift-off. That is my favorite part about flying.

"Here we go!" I exclaimed as we left the ground and into the air. Sam was also holding on for dear life. "Sam, are you scared?" I asked. "No, no, I'm just getting used to change in altitude" Sam replied, just as our ears were popping.

Sam and I stared out the window looking at the land and clouds below. It's so crazy being thirty thousand feet in the air. Imagine the technology and risk that went into making air travel possible. Thank goodness for the Wright brothers.

It wasn't too long before we made it to Florida, when we heard the captain over the loud speaker announcing our arrival in Tampa, Florida. Hubert is waiting for us at the gate, I'm especially excited to see him. It's like seeing your long-lost brother for the first time.

We descended onto the landing strip as the airplane tires screeched on the ground. The plane quickly slowed down as the captain maneuvered to the gate. Everybody stood up to grab their suitcases and backpacks in order to get off the plane. Sam and I were ready to see Hubert and Rella.

It took about fifteen minutes before we could get off the plane and down the aisle to the door. As we got closer, I could see Hubert standing there waiting for us with a big smile on his face. The excitement was building in both Sam and I. We could tell already that this is going to be an amazing time in Florida.

Just as we exited the hallway into the airport, Hubert came up and grabbed Sam and I for a big hug. "I can't believe you guys made it to Florida" Hubert said. He could barely contain his excitement. "It's good to see you brother" I exclaimed. "This is freaking awesome!" Sam replied. "Do we need to go to baggage claim?"

Hubert asked. "No, we both have our packs with us, this is everything we traveled with" I replied.

"I have so much to show you guys!" Hubert said. "Well we're excited to be here. Sam and I are looking forward to all the fun," I replied. "I can't wait to go to the beach and swim in the ocean," Sam added. Hubert replied, "Well, Rella and I will make sure you two have the time of your lives while you are here.

We left the airport and into the parking garage to find Hubert's car. Sam and I immediately got hit with a swarm of humidity as we entered the outside. "Wow, the humidity is thick" I exclaimed. "Woo, yes, it is" Sam added. "You both will get used to the humidity and the heat as the days go by.

It wasn't too long before Hubert pointed the car out. It is a tan two-door Pontiac. It looked really fast. "Let's put your packs in the trunk" Hubert said as he opened the trunk. We put our packs in the car and got inside.

"By the way, I don't have air conditioning" Hubert said with a big laugh. "That's ok, we will definitely drive with the windows down" I replied. I can't believe we are in Tampa, Florida. Who knew this could've ever happened?

Sam and I kept our eyes peeled to the outside of the car. The scenery was amazing. We had never seen so much water and so many bridges. It's as if the entire city is floating on the water. "Wow, this is beautiful" I said. "Just wait until we take you two to Clearwater Beach.

The water is very warm, and the sand is soft as can be." Hubert replied.

Thirty minutes had gone by as we entered Clearwater, Florida. The first thing I noticed was all the retirement homes, apartments and trailer parks. "You weren't kidding when you said the city is full of snow birds" I said to Hubert. "They're everywhere in Clearwater. The retirement community makes up a good portion of the population here" Hubert replied.

"Alright guys, here we are" Hubert said as he drove into an apartment complex on Sunset Point Drive. We pulled right in and parked. As we were getting out of the car, the first thing I notice was all the sand everywhere, but also all the salamanders running around on the ground.

I asked Hubert, "Are these lizards out here all the time?" "Yes, they are. It's one of the coolest things to see around here," Hubert replied. "We also get cockroaches, so we have to keep the apartment extra clean to avoid getting them inside." He added.

Just as I was pre-occupied with the lizards, Rella came walking out of the apartment. "Hey guys! How are you? Isn't this amazing?" Rella asked. "Oh my gosh, give us a hug" I replied. Rella is very cool. She loves the beach, and it shows. Tan arms and legs with bright blonde hair. You could tell she has been to the beach quite a bit.

Hubert and Rella have been together for over a decade. They met in Spokane before moving to Florida. Just like Sam and I, they too were looking for a better life, where the grass is greener on the other side. Instead of grass, they got beach sand. I've been jealous that they could get out of Spokane first.

"You guys bring your packs inside. We have the extra bedroom set up for you both" Hubert stated. "We're going to Clearwater Beach today, so go get into your swimming shorts" Rella added. "Sounds good to us, we are super excited to go to a real beach." I exclaimed.

Sam and I took our packs inside to the extra room and quickly changed into our swimming shorts. Rella gathered up the beach towels while Hubert filled a small cooler with some drinks. "We'll get something to eat at the beach. They have amazing hot dogs" Hubert added.

We all gathered into the car and drove towards Clearwater Beach. It's been said that Clearwater Beach is one of the top ten beaches in the world. Sam and I are totally looking forward to this. We arrived in no time at all. Hubert and Rella live very close to the beach. This explains why they are there all the time.

Hubert pulled into the parking lots and paid the parking meter. I for once can't believe that they charge for parking at the beach. Just another way for the local government to make money off of beachgoers. With sandals on our feet and smiles on our faces, we headed towards the beach.

There was white sand and beach umbrellas as far as our eyes could see. I couldn't believe the amount of people are at the beach. I couldn't wait to go swimming.

We quickly found a space on the beach and laid out our towels to save our spots.

"Let's get in the water" Hubert said with excitement. "Let's go!" I replied. We all ran into the water. Sam and I couldn't believe it. It was like bath water; it was so warm. The Gulf of Mexico is amazing. The water is perfect for swimming all day. I couldn't believe it took me this long to come to Florida, but now we are here.

Chapter 11

Working in the Sunshine State

It didn't take long for the Florida sun to become less of a novelty and more of a hot mess. The humidity swarms you like a big hot hug. The attack squirrels and palmetto bugs became a daily nuisance. Sam and I were really shocked to see loud, flying cockroaches.

Our wardrobe consisted of t-shirts and shorts. Nobody wore pants or long-sleeved shirts in Clearwater, Florida. Carpet didn't exist in any of the homes because of all the sand. You really couldn't go anywhere without tracking in sand on the bottoms of your shoes.

Everybody mostly went to the beach a lot. Other times we were at the bar. One good thing is there were bars on every corner. Florida people loved to drink, especially after a hard day's work. It's work itself that Sam and I want to find. We have plenty of money, but that never lasts long. It's always important to always find a way to keep the money coming in.

Sam and I felt it was time to find some work. "Hey Hubert, where is a good place to find some work?" I asked. "You can come to work with me at North American Van Lines as a mover. We're always looking for workers. The best part is that you can work cash jobs for daily pay," Hubert replied.

"Is it ok if we go with you tomorrow?" Sam asked. "You bet; we'll have plenty of work for you both to do. It's hard work, but I know you guys can do it. I'll call Bob, who is my boss, and let him know you both will be joining the team," Hubert replied.

It was settled. Sam and I could obtain work while we stay here in Florida. Who know how long we will stay? It could be weeks or months before we feel the need to move on. I don't particularly like cold weather, so I'm up for staying as long as we can.

The next day came early. We all woke up around six in the morning to get ready for a hard day's work. Rella cooked us all breakfast. "Here you go boys" Rella said as she sat a plate full of food down on the table. "Eat up and get to work" Rella added. We all ate quick, just so we wouldn't be late for work. We finished up and headed out.

Hubert drove us all to the truck yard at North American Van Lines. We were greeted by Bob. He was the Operations Manager of the company. "Hello gentlemen, welcome to North American Van Lines," Bob stated. "Bob, I would like you to meet Kyler and Sam. They just arrived here from Spokane, Washington. They're ready to work hard" Hubert stated. "Hi Bob, nice to meet you," I added. "It's good to meet you," Sam said.

"Alright guys, you're first job today is a move out for John Lynch, the football player. Stay safe and us the proper lifting techniques. John has a lot of big heavy furniture." Bob said. "We'll take care of it Bob, you will not be disappointed," Hubert replied.

John Lynch lived in a gated community with an armed state patrol man that checked us in at the gate. It was a very protected community. A lot of important people live in the community. Besides John Lynch, there was General Norman Schwarzkopf from the original Gulf War. That's how important their safety is. The State Patrol man did not joke around. He checked all of our identification and searched under the moving truck for anything crazy.

We got through security and made our way to John Lynch's home. It was a huge home with enormous furniture inside and out. We all hopped out of the truck to begin our work. "Alright Kyler and Sam, I want you to

follow me and I will guide you through this move out"
Hubert stated. "Sounds good to us" I replied.

Hubert took us throughout the entire home
pointing at items that need to be padded up and moved
out into the moving truck. Sam and I started picking
items up, either with our bare hands or with a two-wheel
furniture dolly. It didn't take long for the both of us to
sweat our asses off.

Moving a person in the Florida heat was no joke.
Our shirts became soaked with sweat and our hands
became slippery. "Here, put these gloves on" Hubert said
"Thanks bro" I replied. "Yeah thanks bro" Sam added.
The gloves really did help to make sure none of the items
slipped out of our hands.

This move out really broke us in to the moving
business. There were six guys here, and we already knew
this was going to be a twelve-hour job. We have to wraps
and tape furniture pads on virtually everything. Two guys
padded everything while the other four of us moved
them out into the moving truck.

After everything is padded and moved into the
truck, then the truck drives to its final destination to the
clients' new home. Over the next month, we would move
just about every type of person from small loads to big
loads, from two hours to twelve hours. One good thing
is, Sam and I were building some serious muscle. You
definitely don't need a gym membership when you are
working as a mover.

Hubert was a great teacher. He made sure that we
learned everything on every move and also, he taught us

how things work back at the warehouse, especially when it came to moving and storing military moves inside the warehouse. The military moves took the longest because we had to store their belongings inside the warehouse until we were told where the belongings were going. This process could take up to a month from the move out date before it could be moved in to their new base or housing.

Our nights were filled with so much fun. We took our days off seriously. Rella always made sure that the house was clean and our bellies were full of food. She was an amazing host to Sam and I. Rella made it a point to make sure we felt welcome in their home. She also had to put up with our fun drinking nights. Hubert, Sam and I really did like our beer after a hard day's work or just on our days off.

During the days that there was no work at North American Van Lines, Sam and I took up part time work at a furniture warehouse store. We would unload trucks of brand-new furniture and store it in the warehouse. We would also put the furniture together and stage it out on the showroom floor. The owner of the store, Skip, really liked that we worked hard all the time. Because we were from Washington state, we had to prove that we were very hard workers compared to the locals.

Right now, I don't think life could get any better for Sam and I. We decided to stay in Florida for an extended amount of time. There was no reason to go anywhere else right now. We even went down to the

DMV and got our Florida Driver's License. It felt good to be considered and actual resident of Florida.

After a few months of the moving business, Sam and I were looking for another money-making opportunity in Florida. The manual labor of lumping furniture up and down stairs and into and out of the truck, was starting to wear on the both of us. We weren't afraid of hard work; it was just becoming tiring.

First, we quit the furniture warehouse gig. Skip understood, plus he had other workers coming into the warehouse to help and they were pretty loud, which is something Sam and I didn't like. We liked to work in peace and not have our eardrums exploded by people who yell when they talk.

We looked all over for a new job, when Hubert found an ad in the newspaper for cab drivers with no experience necessary. This even intrigued Hubert enough to quit his job at the moving yard to go drive a cab with Sam and I. It appears we all need a break from lumping heavy stuff all over the place.

Hubert said, "Let's go down to Yellow Cab tomorrow and fill out the application." Sam and I were both up for it. All we would have to do is drive a car and take people from one place to another. We would also get good tips if we do an exceptional job.

The next day came and Hubert, Sam and I all drove down to Yellow Cab to fill out our applications. It was a pretty easy process. We were all accepted in as new drivers, but we had to go through some training first. Part of the training was in the classroom and the other part of the training was going with another cab driver as a ride-along so we could see in real time how the driving process works. It also gave us the opportunity to see how the communication equipment works.

The training was really easy. It literally took one day to complete. The basis of the training was all about safety and awareness. We understood the risks we are taking by being a cab driver, including getting robbed by the person we are giving ride to. It doesn't happen that often, but it happens.

One of the most important parts of driving a cab is the cleanliness of the cab. Your car must be cleaned daily. There is a full-service car wash just down the street from Yellow Cab's headquarters. It's always a good idea to have car freshener hanging from your rear-view mirror.

Hubert and Sam drove a Ford Crown Victoria, and I was able to get a Chevy Lumina with red interior. I really liked that car. My passengers like the cozy and clean feel whenever they got in my cab. Hubert was able to get a fairly new Crown Victoria while Sam received an older model that needed some work to the inside. We all three received the cars in dirty conditions, so it was our job to make them sparkle before we started.

It's crazy driving a cab, when all you have is a book style map. It took a bit of time to find the clients homes. The map would take us to their street, but then we had to look for their address on their house. The bad thing was, in Florida, people did not post their address much on the outside of their homes. I truly did not understand why it was this way.

We would get all kinds of customers from regular folks to gangbangers to the mentally ill. Every once in a while, we would transport blood in coolers or medical supplies from the hospital to private offices and vice versa.

A lot of our pickups where from grocery stores. They're usually short trips that didn't pay much, but they filled the day. We are supposed to charge twenty-five cents per grocery bag, but I chose not to charge the extra money. This would allow the customer to leave me a bigger tip.

Sometimes we would get passengers that want to fit five or six people in the car. I didn't want to turn away the business, so I had them cram themselves into the cab. These riders were usually being picked up from a bar, late at night. Of course, being very accommodating also ended with a big tip. We always made sure everyone got home safe.

During the day, a big part of our money came from the mentally ill patients. We would give them a ride back and forth to their treatment place to their home. These were a daily occurrence that we could count on. It was important to make sure you are in the right place at the right time when the call came through.

Of course, we always tried to get the airport runs. These paid forty dollars each time. The only problem was you were driving back to town with an empty cab. We were not allowed to pick up at the airport because we were Clearwater cab drivers, we could only drop off. The Tampa cab drivers were the only ones able to pick up from the airport.

One of my most memorable rides was with a lady who was in labor. Instead of calling an ambulance, she called a cab. You better believe I was driving a little faster to get her to the hospital. Luckily, she did not give birth in my cab. I got her to the hospital on time.

The ones that would irritate me where the drug buying customers. They would have me drive to the bad neighborhood for some meth or coke, then drive them back home. It could get scary at times. Right when we pulled up, we would be swarmed by dealers asking if we wanted to buy marijuana, cocaine or meth. I always kept my window rolled up while the passenger made a deal for what they wanted.

We were told by our supervisors that if the area was too dark or we felt unsafe, we could reject the call. There were a couple times that Hubert would call me and ask me to drive behind him if the customers in his cab were acting suspicious or if he felt like he was going to get robbed. Cab drivers really risk their lives every day to transport people to and from their destinations.

Chapter 12

Life Changes Instantly

All three of us have been making good money being cab drivers. We would give it our all from six o'clock in the morning until the bars closed. A lot of times, we would take a nap during the day when it is slow. This would allow us to be awake and have the energy to do the bar rush later that night.

We met a lot of cool people. Mostly the ones who liked to party. Sam and I each found ourselves in situations where our passenger may or may not have stayed the night with us. Wink, wink, nudge, nudge, if you know what I mean.

It was just too easy to meet people who took a liking to a cab driver that makes two to three hundred dollars per day. The money flowed in and the parties were a plenty. Of course, the both of us have a couple regrets here and there, thanks to our beer goggles. It gave us something to laugh about later.

One of the coolest events happened when Hubert and Rella introduced Sam and I to a rock band named Skin Deep. They were starting their tour of Florida when they asked Hubert, Sam and I to be their official drivers from gig to gig. Hubert and I also became their light and sound guys, while Sam sold their awesome shirts at each concert.

The band was popular in the Clearwater and Tampa area so much so that their concerts would sell out each night. We almost lost the transportation job when Sam slept with the lead singer's wife until she convinced her husband that nothing happened. They were going through a divorce so it was kind of ok and kind of not ok.

Mostly, the good outweighed the bad when driving a cab. The money was just too easy. If we needed anything, we would just go drive for a few hours until we made the money that we needed.

For most of the job, we made a lot of great friends. We would constantly be invited to parties or get togethers. When you are the driver, everybody needs you. Sometimes we would give free rides to our close friends.

Sam and I were also able to find some side jobs along the way. Because of our experience and know how, we booked a job from a retiree that needed their trailer gutted and remodeled. We loved work like that. It was kind of fun.

It took us about a month to complete the job. We did a lot of work for one thousand dollars each. The customer was extremely happy with her new laminate floor and the interior paint job. We made a really cool faux rock wall in her back office. It was the owner's idea; we just did the work.

Between the concerts, the parties, the beach and the overnight guests, we were having the time of our life. Hubert and Rella were the best. They allowed us to stay with them the entire time. They truly didn't want us to leave.

Everything was going well until I met a customer, I wish I hadn't. This guy was a serious character. He was always about the business and never the fun. Sam and I would both pick up this guy on separate occasions. His drive would always freak us out.

We couldn't figure out if he was selling drugs or just plain killing people. He was always in and out, with the rides being round trip. Sam and I knew that when we picked him up, we were going to get a nice tip. For some reason, this guy would tip us great as long as we kept our mouths shut.

Then one day, the guy spoke up. I was driving when he called me on my cell phone. He said it was important that I picked him up right now. I didn't have any other passengers, so I went right over to pick him up.

The man always met us at a restaurant, and never his actual home. I didn't think anything of it this time. Everything was going as normal, at least I thought. This time the ride was a lot different.

I picked him up and asked him, "Where are we going tonight," He responded, "I need to go to Office Depot." I thought nothing of it and said, "Absolutely, I know exactly where Office Depot was. I didn't even have to use my map.

It didn't take too long before we reached Office Depot, just off of the freeway. I pulled into the parking lot and drove as close as I could to the front doors when he added, "I need you to park by the entrance to the parking lot with your car facing towards the driveway."

I was sure what was going on, but I knew that this was a very odd request. I parked where he instructed me to park. He said, "Wait right here, I'll be right out." "Alright, sounds good" I replied. The man got out of the cab, leaving my back door slightly open and walked into Office Depot.

Only fifteen minutes went by, when suddenly, the man came running towards my cab. He jumped in with a laptop in hand and yelled, "Go! Go! Go! It freaked me out so bad, I put the pedal to the metal and sped off before he even had a chance to close his door.

I sped off onto the freeway without even looking to see if it was safe to enter traffic. I asked him, "What just happened?" He was honest with me, "I just stole this laptop!" "What! Are you serious?" I asked. "Yes, I grabbed the laptop and walked up to the counter acting like I was going to buy it. Then as they were ringing up the purchase, I grabbed the laptop and ran out the door." He replied.

I could not believe it! This man just stole a laptop from Office Depot and used me as a getaway vehicle. I wanted to get off the road as fast as possible. I asked him "Where am I taking you?" "Take me to the restaurant as usual. We will park in back until the buyer arrives" He replied.

Evidently, this man steals laptops and sells them for drugs. We went to the restaurant and parked. I was still freaking out as my heart was pounding non-stop. Then a car pulled up next to me. The man rolled down the window and handed the laptop to the man in the car next to us. The buyer handed the man three hundred dollars and drove away.

The man handed me one hundred dollars for my time as he exited the vehicle. "I'll call you again" the man said. "Ok, talk to you later" I replied. I said that knowing full well that I would never answer his call again. I appreciated the one hundred dollars, but that was too risky for me. I immediately drove home and parked the cab for the night.

I told Hubert and Sam what had happened. They also advised me to never answer his call again. That was just too crazy for my liking. We all three blocked his phone number on our cell phones, hoping to never hear from him again.

I went to bed that night praying that nothing would come of it and that I would stay safe. I promised God that if he let me off on this one, that I would do nothing like that again. My prayers were answered. I never received a call from the police and nobody identified my cab as the getaway car. I was safe from any harm.

From there on out, I walked the straight and narrow path of safety and sobriety. There was no reason ever that any amount of money was ever going to be big enough to have me take part in any suspicious activity with anybody.

Time went on for Hubert, Rella, Sam and I. Times were still fun in Florida. Sam and I contemplated staying longer through the winter. It sounded like a great idea. Hubert and Rella were more than accommodating with us both. They allowed us to stay as long as we wanted.

We just carried on with our normal cab driving life, except this time we are staying out of trouble. We had a good thing going and plenty of regular passengers that called us on our cell phones instead of us having to log on to the dispatch radio.

It was a typical Friday night when Hubert, Sam and I took off in our cabs to take advantage of the weekenders going to and from the bars. We had our regulars calling us back to back needing rides. It was a very lucrative night that produced a lot of cash in our pockets.

Sometimes we can get too comfortable with people we knew. The people we thought we could trust. The people whom we thought would never hurt us. Yes indeed, we got to comfortable.

I was waiting on the main strip for calls when I received a call from Hubert. "Hey bro, please be careful right now. I just got word that one of our fellow cab drivers just got robbed. You should call Sam to let him know you both should call it a night and come home. I'm on my way home as we speak," "Alright bro, I will call Sam right now," I replied.

I called Sam, but there was no answer. His phone didn't even ring, just straight to voicemail. That never happens, Sam always answers his phone to me, even if he is driving. After calling five times, I figured something must be wrong or his phone battery went dead.

I thought, well maybe I'll drive over to his regular spot by the Diamond Dolls strip club. I started my car and off I headed in his direction. It took about fifteen minutes for me to get to the club. As I approached the club, I could see flashing lights from police cars, fire trucks and an ambulance.

My heart immediately started racing as I see a burned-out cab surrounded by the first responders. I pulled in to the other side of the parking lot and got out of my cab. I ran over knowing the cab looked just like Sam's.

To my surprise, it was Sam's cab. But where is Sam? I approached a police officer. "That's my friends cab! Where is Sam?" The police officer told me to stand back. "No! That's my friends cab, where is Sam?" I asked again. I could see there was no one in the driver's seat.

"You know the driver of the cab?" The officer asked. "Yes, he is my best friend. We drive cab together." "Ok, please calm down," the officer asked. "I will calm down when you tell me where my friend is. He won't even answer his phone," I exclaimed.

The officer replied "He can't answer his phone sir. I'm sorry to have to tell you this, but your friend Sam is dead. He was the victim of an armed robbery. The robber stabbed Sam in the back, slit his throat, put Sam's body in the trunk and set the car on fire. The body is burned beyond any recognition,"

I burst into tears and fell to the ground. "What! No! No! No! This can't be happening. Sam is my best friend. Why? Why? Why?" The officer replied, "We confirmed with the cab company that Sam was driving this cab. I'm so sorry, sir. Is there someone I can call for you to pick you up?"

"No! I can take care of myself" I'm trembling and crying uncontrollably as I get into my cab. I drive as fast as I could go get back to Hubert and Rella's. I burst through the door and fall to my knees. "He's dead, he's dead, Sam is dead!" I screamed. "What happened!" Hubert asked.

I told Hubert and Rella everything the officer told me. "I don't want to drive cab anymore!" I screamed. "I can't do this; I just can't do this anymore" I added. Hubert and Rella consoled me as much as possible. We were all three in tears and disbelief.

I sat on the sofa reflecting on my friendship with Sam. Everything we did together including our amazing traveling experiences. Sam can never be replaced. I will miss him every day. If I hadn't asked him to travel with me, he would still be alive today. I feel totally responsible for my best friend's death.

Chapter 13

The Priest

My heart is broken. The level of sadness cannot even be measured right now. It's as if time has stood still and I can barely breathe. My tears are non-stop and my life has been turned upside down. What do I do? Where can I go? The answer is nothing, nothing can replace the friend I have lost.

Sam didn't deserve to die. He was literally the nicest guy in the world. No faults could be brought against him. I am lost and I can't even find myself. Hubert and Rella are right there by my side. They also have lost a friend. Our home has lost a soul. We all feel empty inside.

Hubert and I are done with driving a cab. The risk is no longer worth it. We turned in our cabs to the depot with Rella waiting to take us home. Life will never be the same. Sam's life was just getting started. He was only twenty years old.

I honestly don't know what to do or where to turn. Where is my life going now? I'm stuck without a purpose. Do I stay in Florida or do I back home to Spokane? My thoughts are racing around in my head with no end in sight.

I went to my bedroom for some alone time. For now, I need to be alone to think through what I should do. I love Hubert and Rella, but I need some time alone. If I leave, they will be in shock, but they will understand hopefully.

The time has come for me to decide. It's now midnight at Hubert and Rella's house. They are fast asleep, but I am wide awake. I need to make a move and I need to do it right now.

I wrote a long note to Hubert and Rella. I thank them for their hospitality and apologize for what I'm about to do. The basis of the letter is to let them know that I am going back home to clear my thoughts and figure out my life. "I'm going back home to ask the wizard for a new brain." I know that sounds weird, but I literally need to figure out what to do with myself.

The silence of the night is telling me to go. I packed up my belongings, opened the bedroom window and crawled out to the outside. Hopefully my note will explain it all and they will not be mad.

I took my pack of belongings and walked to the nearest convenience store, just a couple blocks away. I sat there on the curb and pulled out my phone. It's time for me to get away. I pulled out my cell phone and called a cab. Imagine that, I am using the service that killed my best friend, in order to get away and go home.

The cab was there within ten minutes. I placed my pack in the backseat with me and sat there quietly. "Please take me to the nearest Greyhound Station" I asked the driver. "No problem sir" The driver replied. Now I was off to a new life. I will grieve Sam in my own way. I need to change what I am doing in life.

It didn't take long at all to arrive at the Greyhound Station. It's not my desired mode of transportation, but something was telling me to take the bus home instead of flying. I definitely need the time on the road to close out this chapter in my life.

I paid the cab driver and sent him on his way. The greyhound station was open, so I walked directly inside to purchase my ticket. It didn't cost too much to buy the ticket home. I still had plenty of money left to last me another month once I got back to Spokane.

There was only one other person in the Greyhound Station. He was and African-American man that stood six foot four inches tall and looked to weigh about three hundred pounds of muscle. I noticed he was watching me the entire time I was getting my ticket and then continued to watch me as I sat in the uncomfortable chair while waiting for the bus to arrive.

He was quiet, but he kept an eye on me for some reason. The next hour had gone by slowly as the bus finally arrived. I grabbed my pack and got in line while the people where coming off the bus. The African-American man stood directly behind me, still keeping his eye on me.

After all the people got off the bus, it was time for me to get on the bus. I showed the driver my ticket and gave him my pack to put underneath the bus in the cargo hold. The man behind me did exactly the same.

I boarded the bus to find a spot with two empty seats near the back of the bus. I quickly sat in the window seat because I like to look out the window while traveling. Wouldn't you know it though, with all the empty seats available, the man that was watching me sat down right next to me. This was very odd and kind of scary at the same time.

My mind was racing with thoughts. Why is he sitting next to me? Why was he staring at me? What does he want from me? I didn't know the answers to these questions, but I'm sure I will find out the answers real soon.

Everybody had boarded the bus as the driver let us know it was time to leave. The driver put his seat belt on and started the bus's engine. "Here we go!" the driver shouted. He is a nice bus driver compared to the ones I had in the past.

We were pulling away from the station when a big calmness came over me. I felt free and safe, but very sad at the same time. I felt something as if Sam was watching over me.

After a couple hours, we came to a stop at another Greyhound station in northern Florida. "You have twenty minutes to be back on the bus" the driver shouted. The man sitting next to me got up to get off the bus. I also needed a break to stretch my legs. I placed my coat in the seat so nobody would take me spot.

I quickly went inside the bus station to use the restroom. As soon as I came out, the man that was sitting next to me approached me. "Hello, how are you?" he asked. "I'm good, just on my way home" I replied.

"You seem like a cool guy, come outside with me" he asked. "Sure, what's up?" I replied. "Just come with me?" Something told me I was safe with him, so I followed him outside. We went around to the back of the bus station by the dumpsters. Nobody else was there. We were both out of sight from the bus or anybody was on the bus.

The man pulled out a pouch from his pocket and opened it up. To my surprise, he pulled out a joint. "You need this right now" the man said. "Oh, heck yes!" I replied. I really needed a joint to take the edge off and calm myself down even more.

"My name is Priest. What's your name?" he asked. "My name is Kyler, it's nice to meet you." I replied. Priest lit up the joint, took a hit, then passed it to me. I took a huge drag before passing it back. "This is great weed" I said. "It's Florida's best" he replied.

Priest could tell there was something wrong with me. He could tell I was sad. "What's your story?" he asked. "My best friend was just murdered in Florida. I'm pretty torn up from it, so I am making my way back home to Spokane, Washington." I replied. "Where are you headed? I asked.

"I'm headed to San Francisco, but something told me to watch over you during this trip. Stay close to me and I will protect you," Priest replied. "Is Priest your real name?" I asked. "No, it's not my real name. I go by Priest because I am a priest for the church of the streets. I teach the gospel of Jesus and help all who are in need," He replied.

"I knew there was something about you I needed to help you and protect you during our time together. I will make sure the lord watches over you," Priest stated. "Thank you so much, I need it right now," I replied.

The joint was at an end and it was time to get back on the bus. We walked around front to the bus and got back in our seats. The bus was now headed to Mississippi. "There is a great place to get something to eat at the Mississippi station. Sit back, relax and I will let you know when we get there" Priest added.

I put my headphones on to listen to some music as Priest closed his eyes to get some sleep. We both started our journey in the middle of the night, so I knew he had to of been tired. I listen to all my favorite songs as the bus rolled on down the highway.

After a while of driving, we pulled into the Mississippi station, which also happened to be right next door to an authentic southern food stop. Priest woke up and advised, "Here we are, let's get something to eat." We all got off the bus, while Priest and I walked over to the food stop.

"This is on me; I'll order for you" Priest said. "Thank you very much, I appreciate your kindness" I replied. "No problem, my brother" Priest ordered alligator, black-eyed peas, collard greens and cornbread. I had never had alligator before, so this will be a new experience for me.

We sat down outside in the humid weather to eat our food. I couldn't believe it, but as we say, the alligator tastes just like chicken. It was so good, I thanked Priest again for this meal. Of course, before we got back on the bus, we had to smoke another joint to keep us at ease on this bus ride.

It really felt like Priest was watching over me and protecting me on this journey home. I felt safe and at ease. We finished the joint and got back on the bus to our seats. Our next destination was Houston, Texas.

Every stop we took, Priest would pull out another joint as we took a stroll through our destinations. We smoke in downtown Houston, The Alamo and our last stop in Texas was El Paso. That was one of my favorite spots, because the Greyhound station was right at the U.S. and Mexico border.

Priest knew some people in El Paso that were working near the bus station. Their line of work reminded me of my mom's old business because the ladies Priest was preaching to were prostitutes.

"Come on Kyler, follow me" Priest asked. We walked right over to the U.S. and Mexico border. We looked out into Mexico to see shacks and makeshift houses. "I feel back for the people in Mexico. You can clearly see and economic difference between the two countries" I stated. I'll never forget smoking a joint and looking out into Mexico from the U.S. border.

It was time for us to get back on the bus. Our next destination was Phoenix, Arizona. It seemed like the humidity was following us through the southern states. I didn't mind the humidity, it was very comfortable and calming, especially after smoking some weed with the guy who is protecting me.

We made our way through Phoenix, Arizona then on to Las Vegas, Nevada. From there we headed into California. Our first stop in California was San Diego. This had two of been the hottest place we stopped at. From there we went to Los Angeles, California. This was probably the most unnerving part of California I had been to. Priest protected me though. I definitely stayed close to him in L.A.

Next, we went on to San Jose and then to Priest's final destination of San Francisco, California. I got off the bus with Priest as he grabbed his bags from underneath. "Thank you for everything you had done for me" I stated. "No problem my brother. It was a pleasure hanging out and smoking with you. Here are a couple joints to get you through until you make it back to Spokane" Priest replied.

"Maybe one day, I'll make it up to Spokane and we can connect once again" Priest added. "Absolutely, that would be awesome" I replied. Priest grabbed his bags and walked on to his next journey. I got back on the bus, awaiting my final destination.

We went on through traveling north on I-5 going throughout California, then on to Portland, Oregon and then onto Seattle, Washington. I was getting closer to my destination. Each stop, I would smoke some more weed to keep my emotions in check and to remember Sam. It seemed that I just wanted to do things in his remembrance.

I was back in Washington and heading east on I-90 towards Spokane. I kept my headphones on playing music that would remind me of Sam. It's going to take a while to get over this feeling, but I will continue to remember Sam as much as possible.

Before I knew it, I was back in Spokane, the familiar view coming down from Airway Heights into downtown took my breath away. No matter how many times, I will never get tired of that view heading east into Spokane. We pulled into the Intermodal Center to the Greyhound and Amtrak station. I got off the bus and grabbed my pack to make my way outside to the front of the building.

I waited there for my friend to come pick me up. She is always late, which is no big deal. It gave me time to smoke one last joint in Sam's memory, before I started my new life. It will be extremely hard because I don't know how long this sadness will last or if I can ever get over it. All I can do is try.

.... It's time for Kyler to seek help

Not the End

An American Son: Kyler's Journey

An American Son: Kyler's Journey

CPSIA information can be obtained
at www.ICGtesting.com
Printed in the USA
BVHW071536071220
595086BV00007B/1029